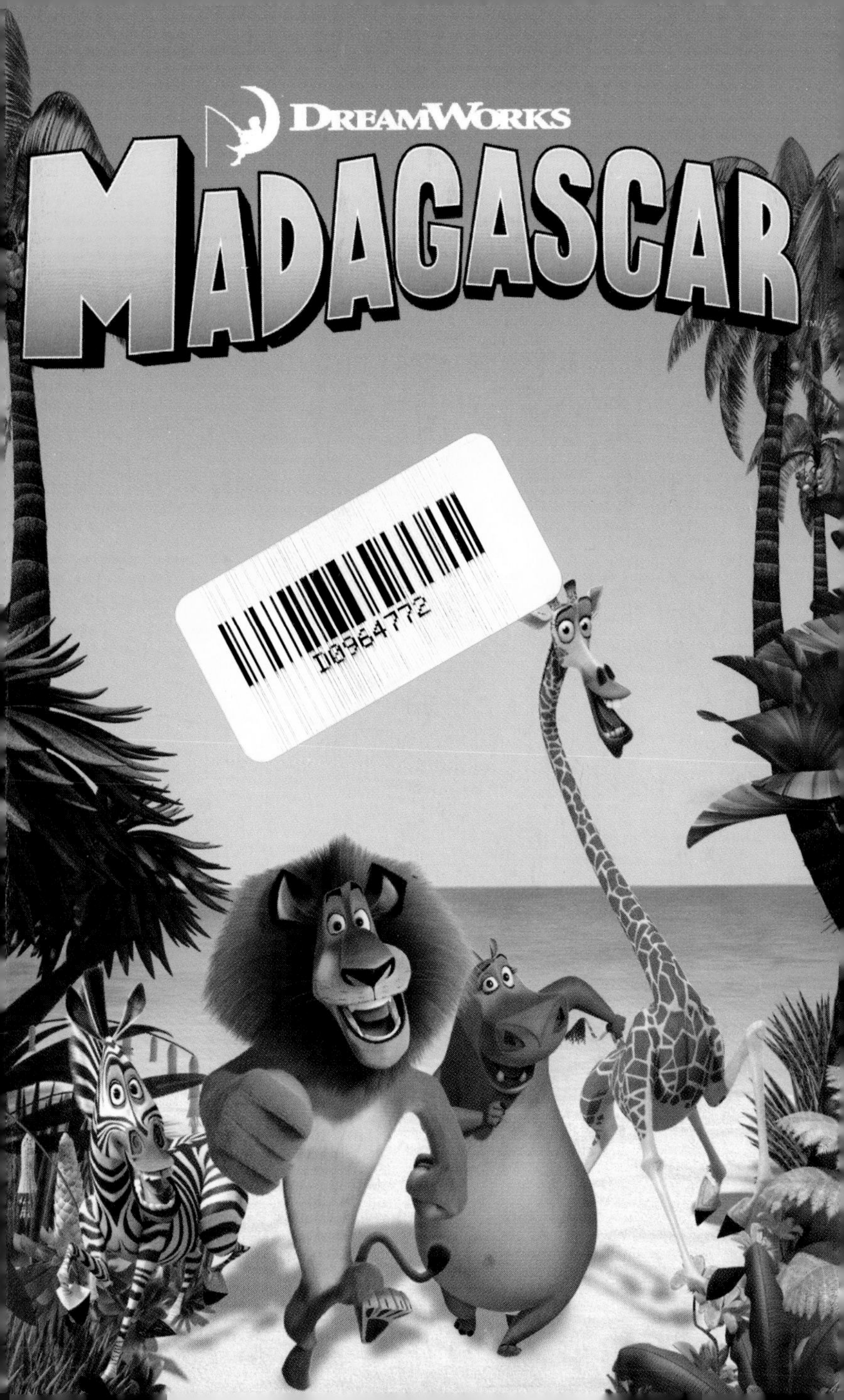
DreamWorks
MADAGASCAR

Editors - Erin Stein and Zachary Rau
Contributing Editor - Amy Court Kaemon
Graphic Designer and Letterer - Rob Steen
Cover Designer - Anna Kernbaum
Graphic Artists - Monalisa J. de Asis, John Lo and Louis Csontos

Digital Imaging Manager - Chris Buford
Production Managers - Jennifer Miller and Mutsumi Miyazaki
Senior Designer - Anna Kernbaum
Senior Editor - Elizabeth Hurchalla
Managing Editor - Jill Freshney
VP of Production - Ron Klamert
Publisher & Editor in Chief - Mike Kiley
President & C.O.O. - John Parker
C.E.O. - Stuart Levy

E-mail: info@TOKYOPOP.com
Come visit us online at www.TOKYOPOP.com

A ⊙ TOKYOPOP® Cine-Manga® Book
TOKYOPOP Inc.
5900 Wilshire Blvd., Suite 2000
Los Angeles, CA 90036

Madagascar

ISBN: 1-59816-376-0

First TOKYOPOP® printing: October 2005

10 9 8 7 6 5 4 3 2 1

Printed in Canada

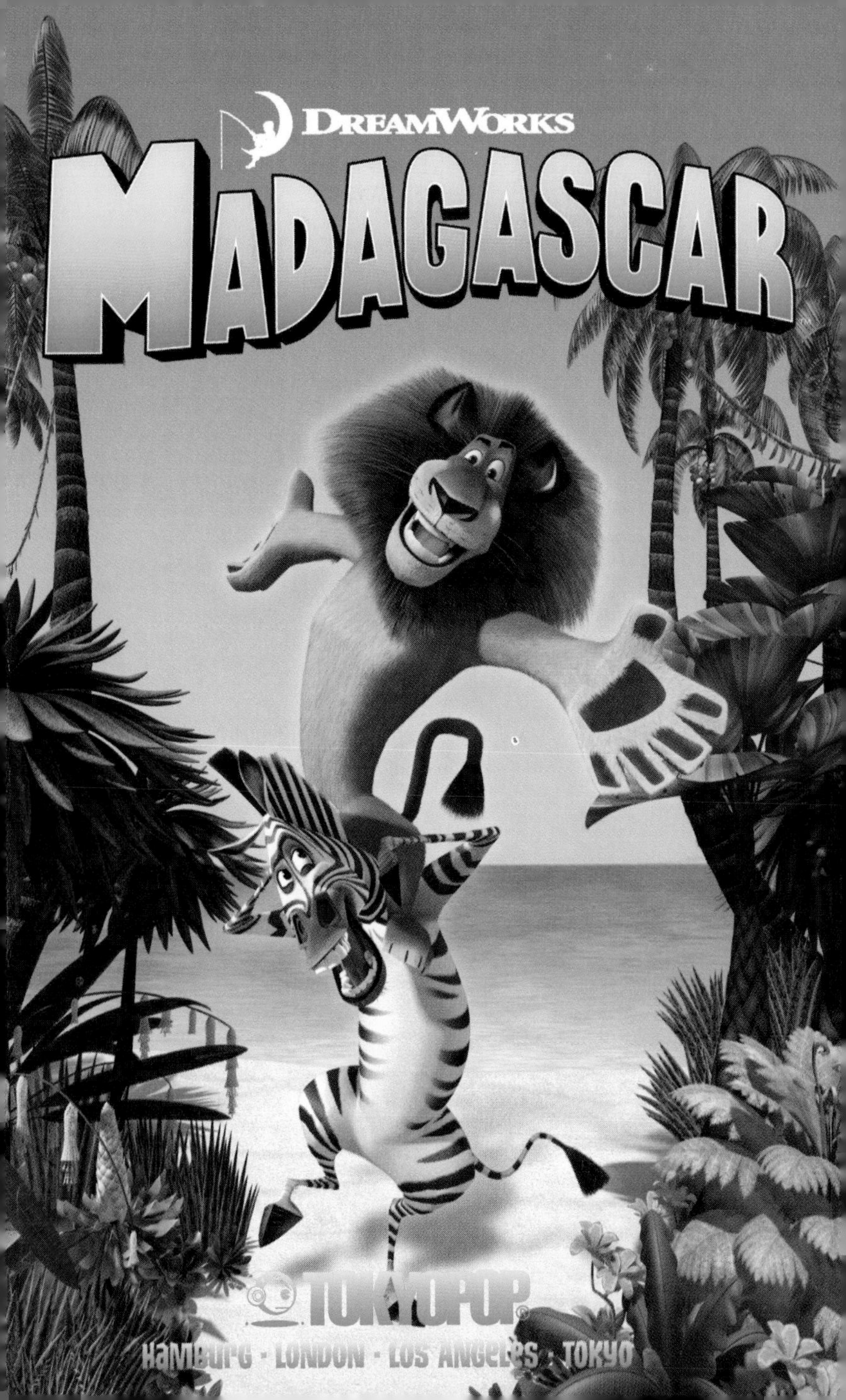
DreamWorks
MADAGASCAR
TOKYOPOP
Hamburg · London · Los Angeles · Tokyo

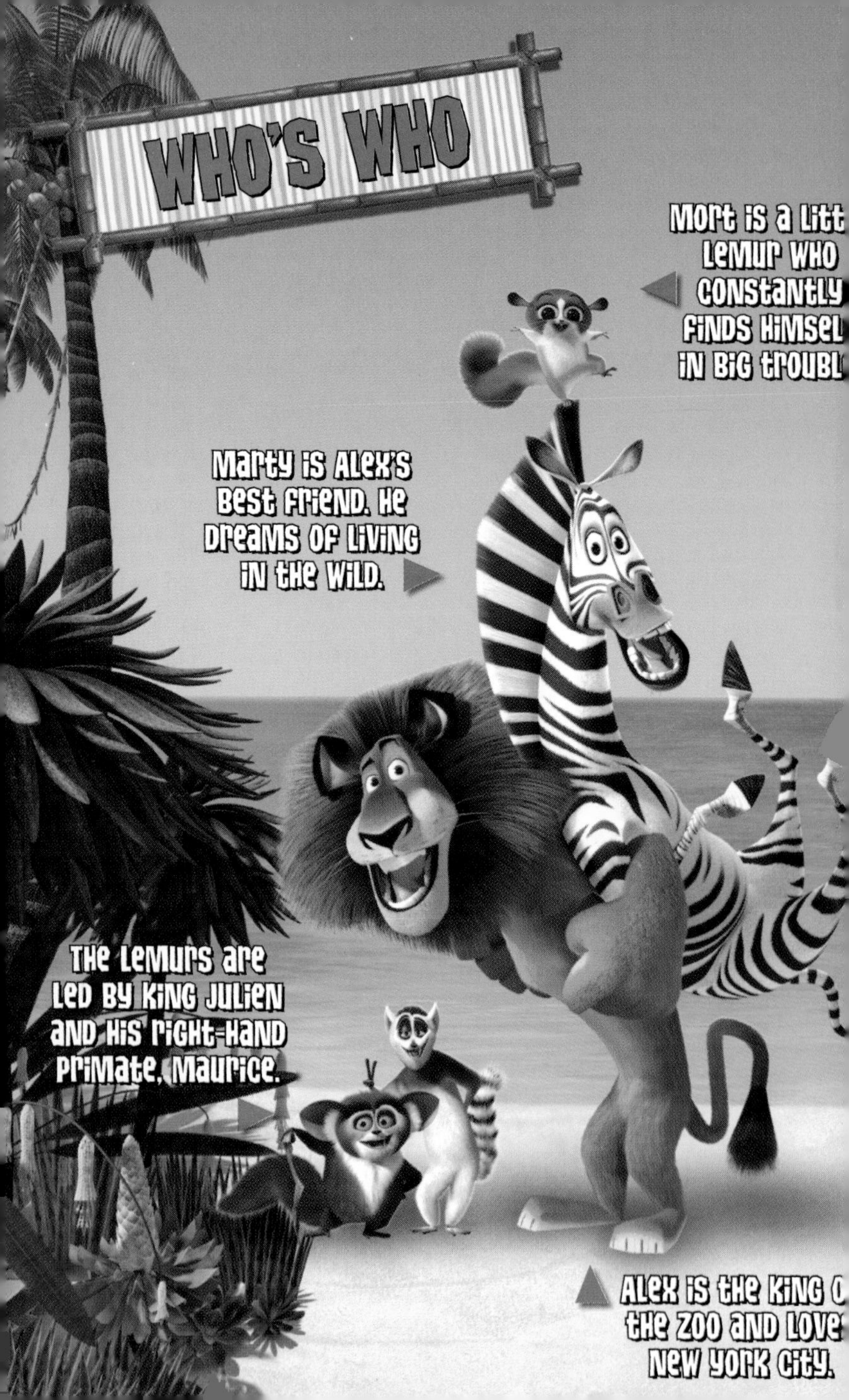
WHO'S WHO
Mort is a Litt Lemur who constantly finds himsel in big troubl
Marty is Alex's best friend. He dreams of living in the wild.
The lemurs are led by King Julien and his right-hand primate, Maurice.
Alex is the king o the zoo and love New York City.

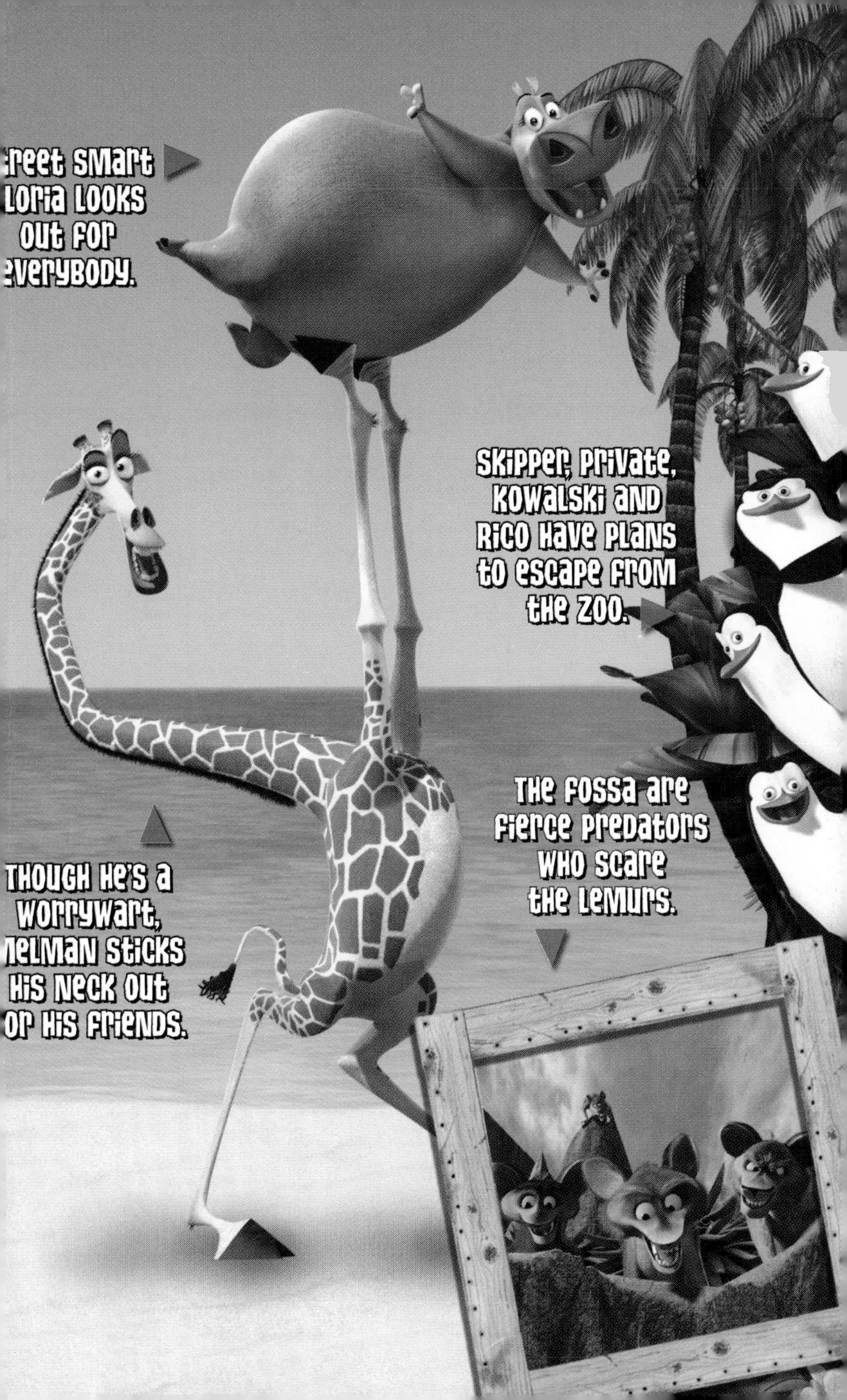

reet Smart
Loria Looks
out for
everybody.
Skipper, Private,
Kowalski and
Rico have plans
to escape from
the zoo.
The fossa are
fierce predators
who scare
the lemurs.
Though he's a
worrywart,
elman sticks
his neck out
or his friends.

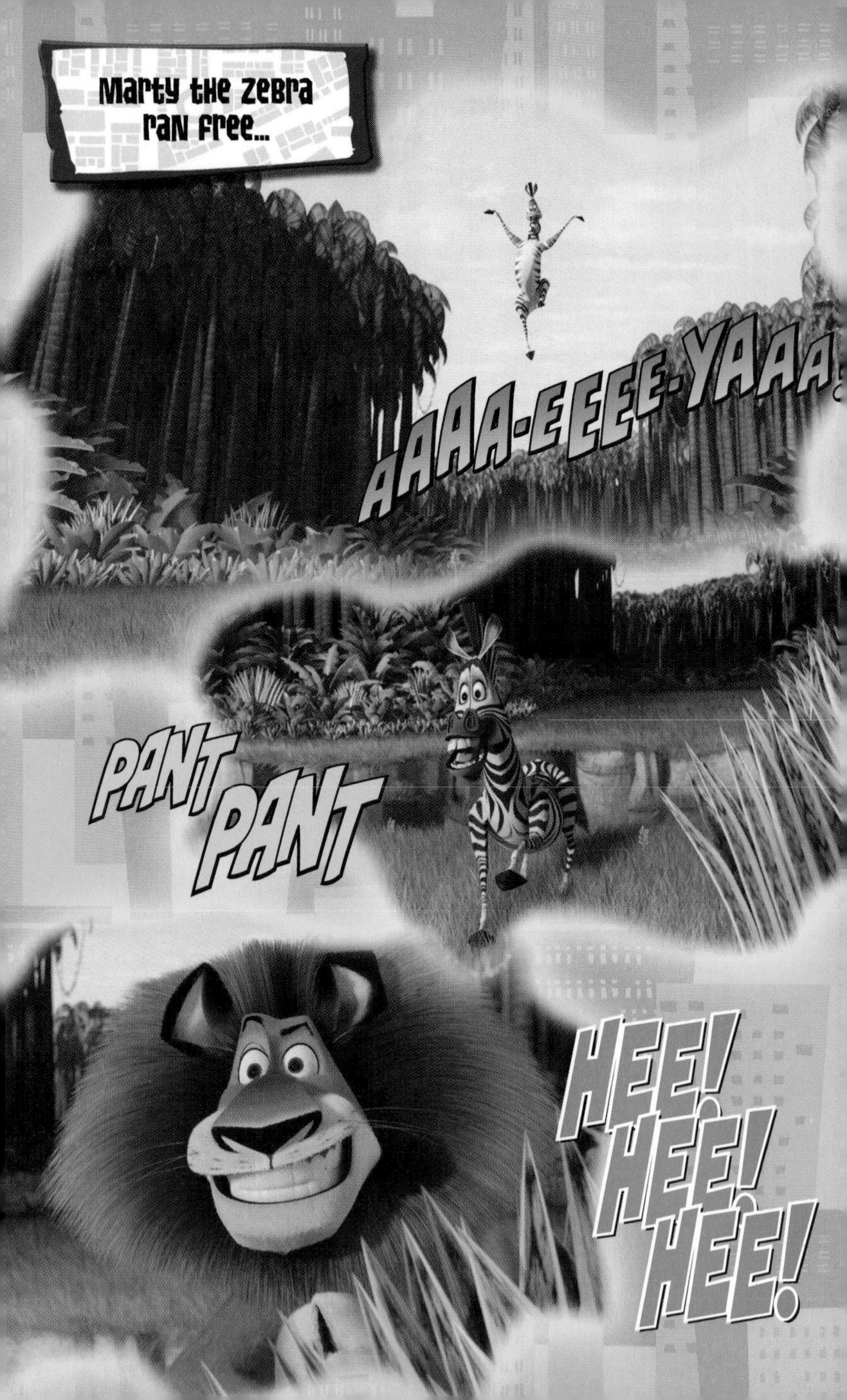
Marty the zebra ran free...
AAAA-EEEE-YAAA!
PANT PANT
HEE! HEE! HEE!

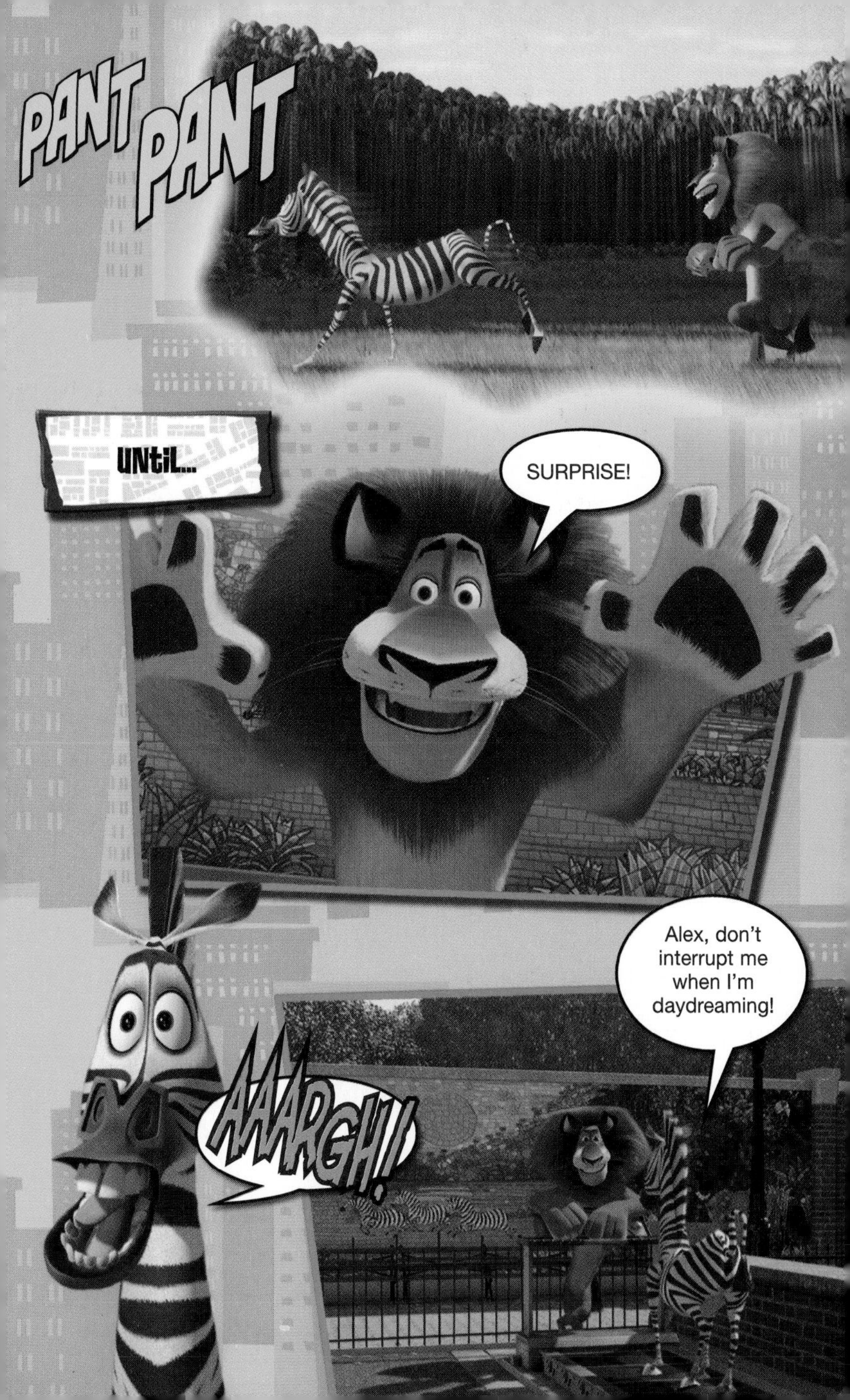
PANT PANT
UNTIL...
SURPRISE!
AAARGH!!
Alex, don't interrupt me when I'm daydreaming!

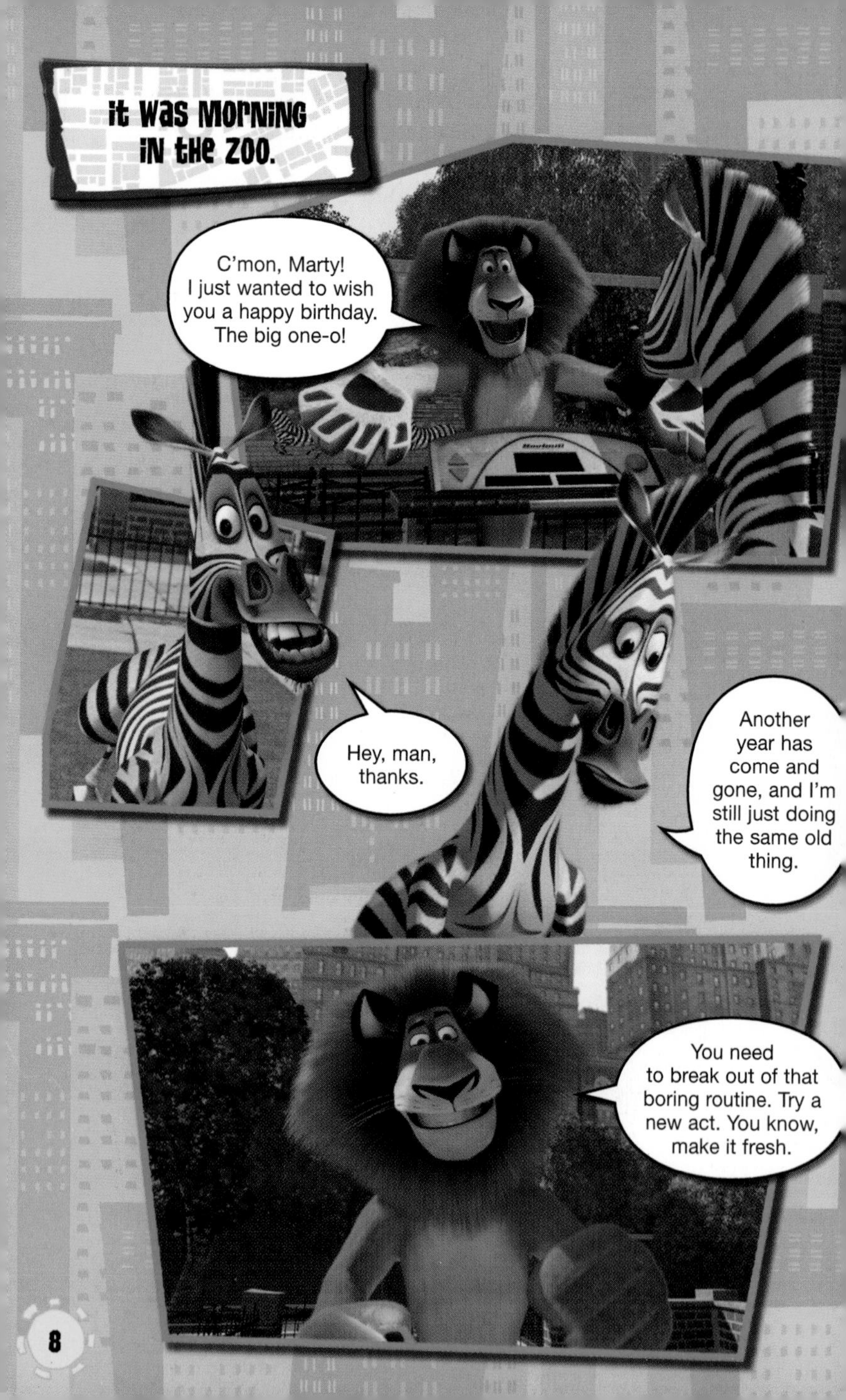
It was morning in the zoo.
C'mon, Marty! I just wanted to wish you a happy birthday. The big one-o!
Hey, man, thanks.
Another year has come and gone, and I'm still just doing the same old thing.
You need to break out of that boring routine. Try a new act. You know, make it fresh.

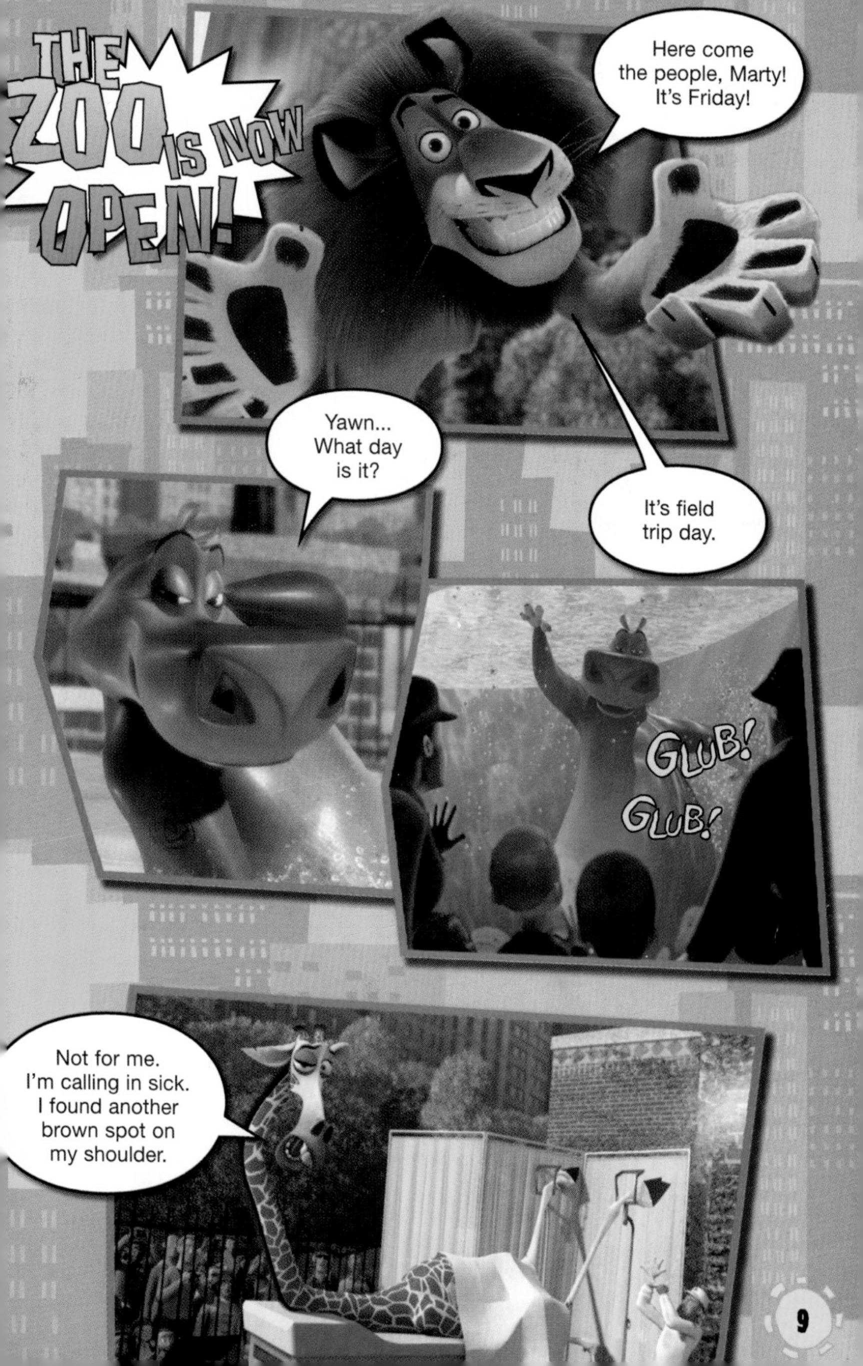
THE ZOO IS NOW OPEN!
Here come the people, Marty! It's Friday!
Yawn... What day is it?
It's field trip day.
GLUB! GLUB!
Not for me. I'm calling in sick. I found another brown spot on my shoulder.

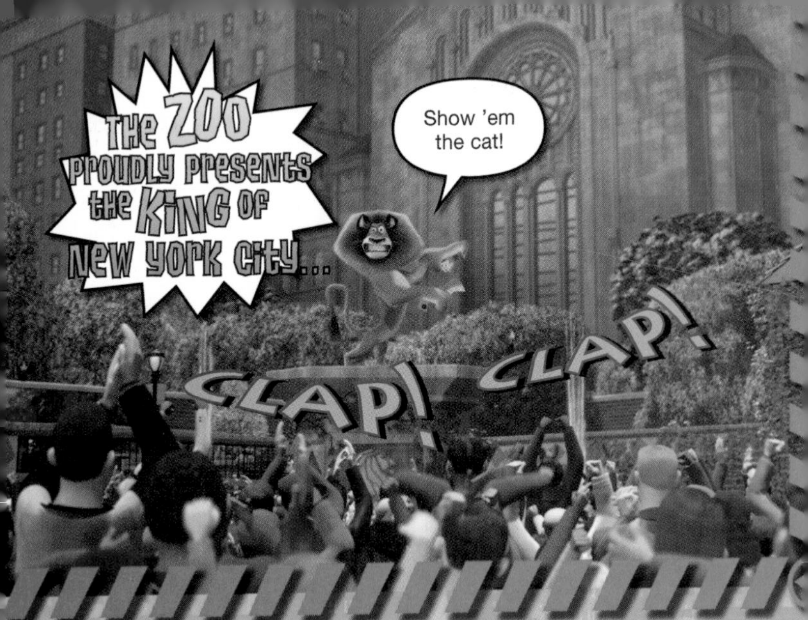
The ZOO proudly presents the KING of New York City...
Show 'em the cat!
CLAP! CLAP!

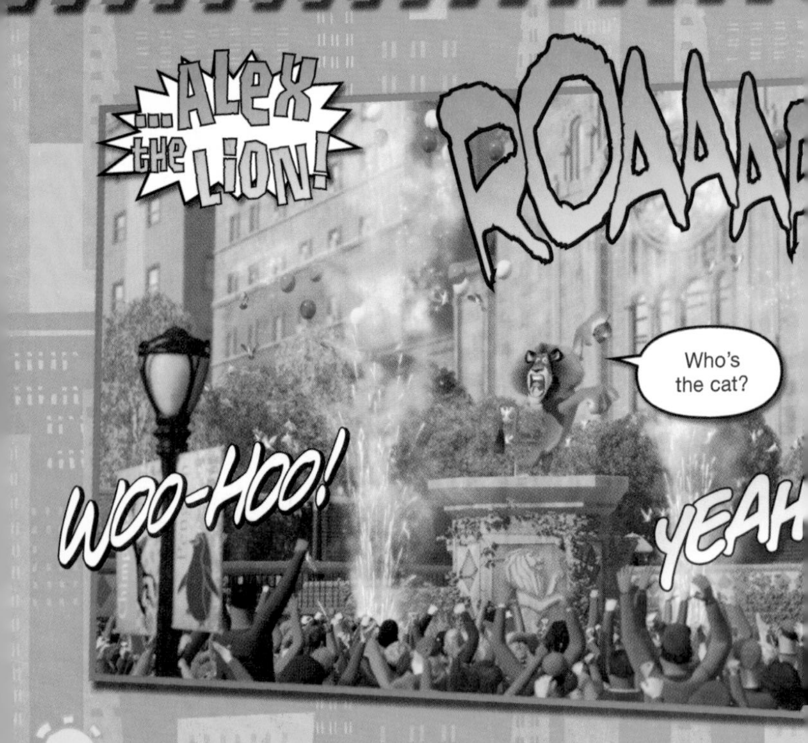
...ALEX the LION!
ROAAA
Who's the cat?
WOO-HOO!
YEAH

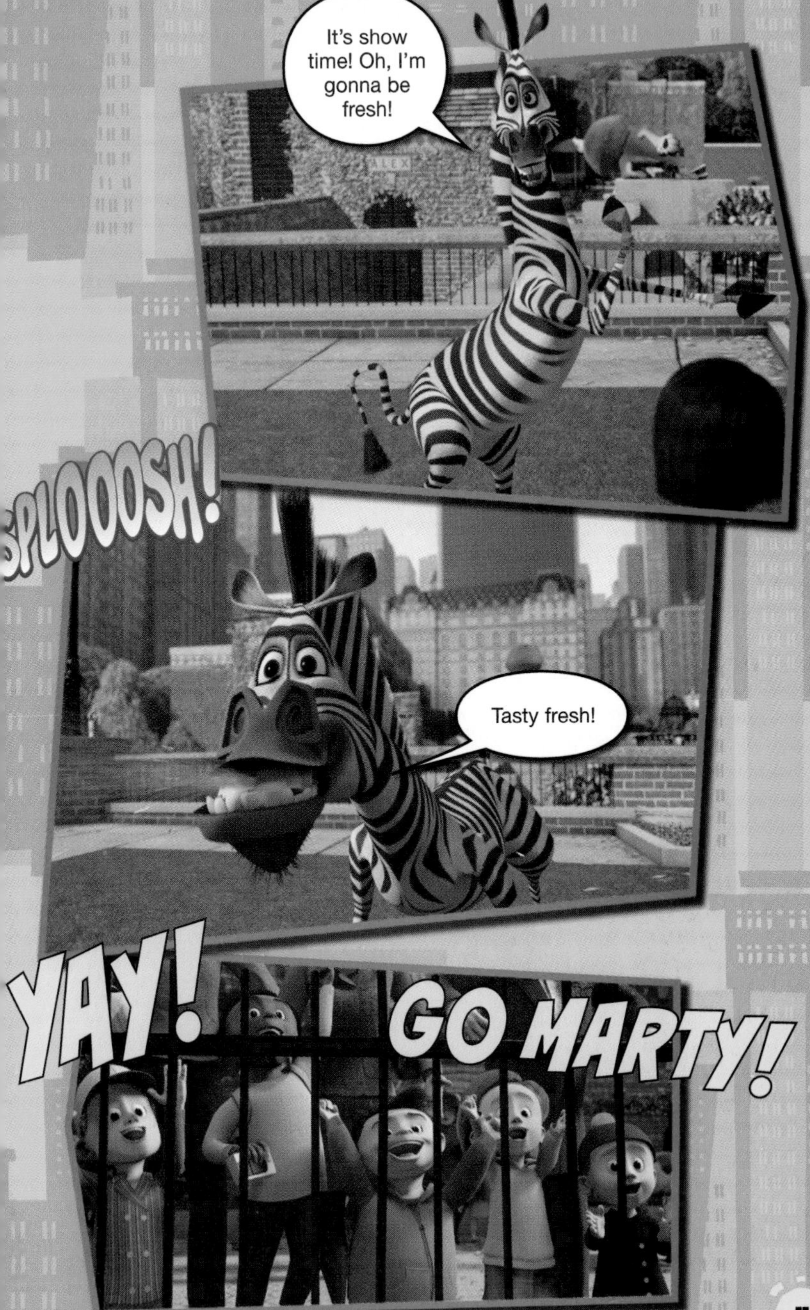
It's show time! Oh, I'm gonna be fresh!
SPLOOOSH!
Tasty fresh!
YAY!
GO MARTY!

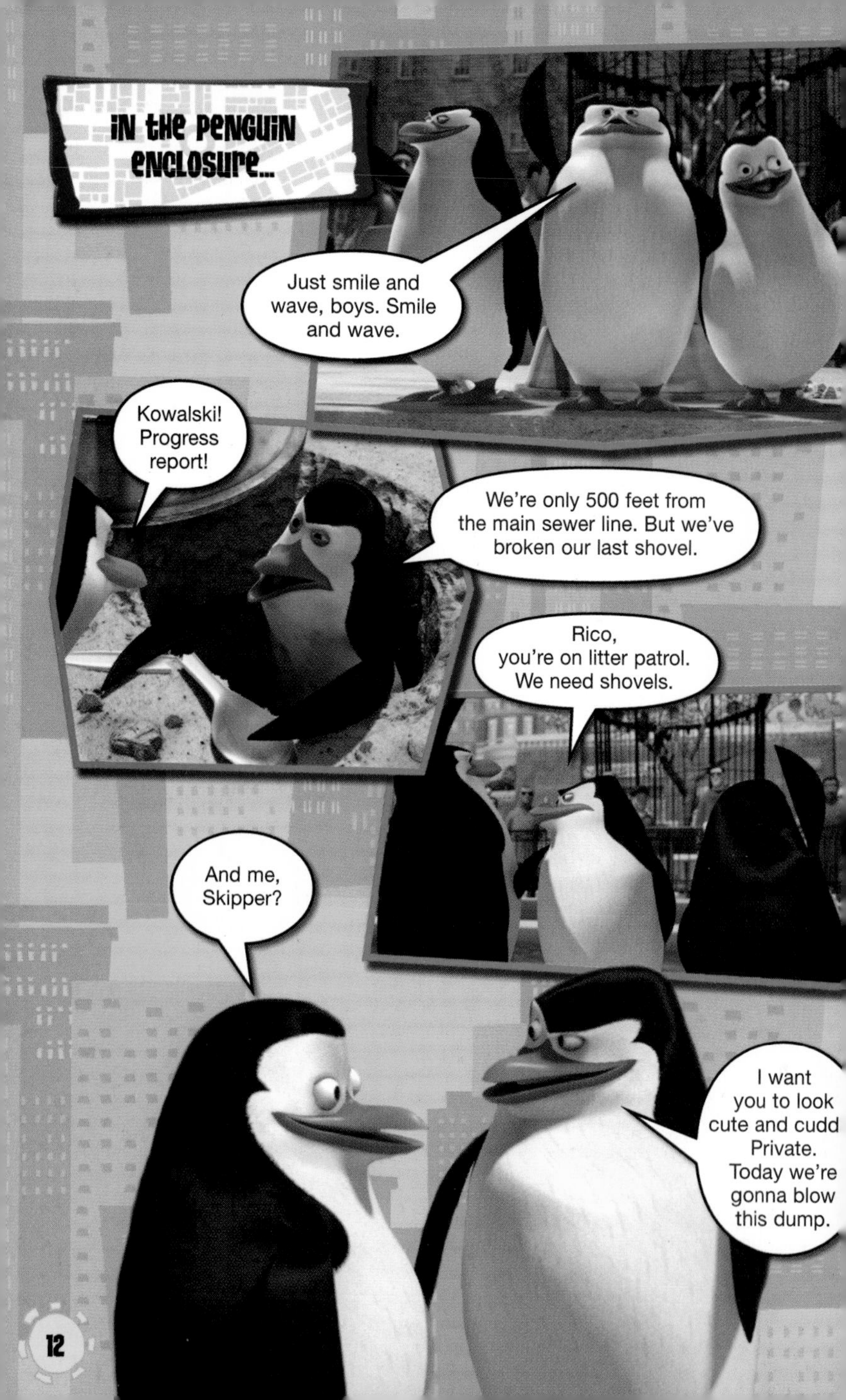
In the Penguin enclosure...
Just smile and wave, boys. Smile and wave.
Kowalski! Progress report!
We're only 500 feet from the main sewer line. But we've broken our last shovel.
Rico, you're on litter patrol. We need shovels.
And me, Skipper?
I want you to look cute and cudd Private. Today we're gonna blow this dump.

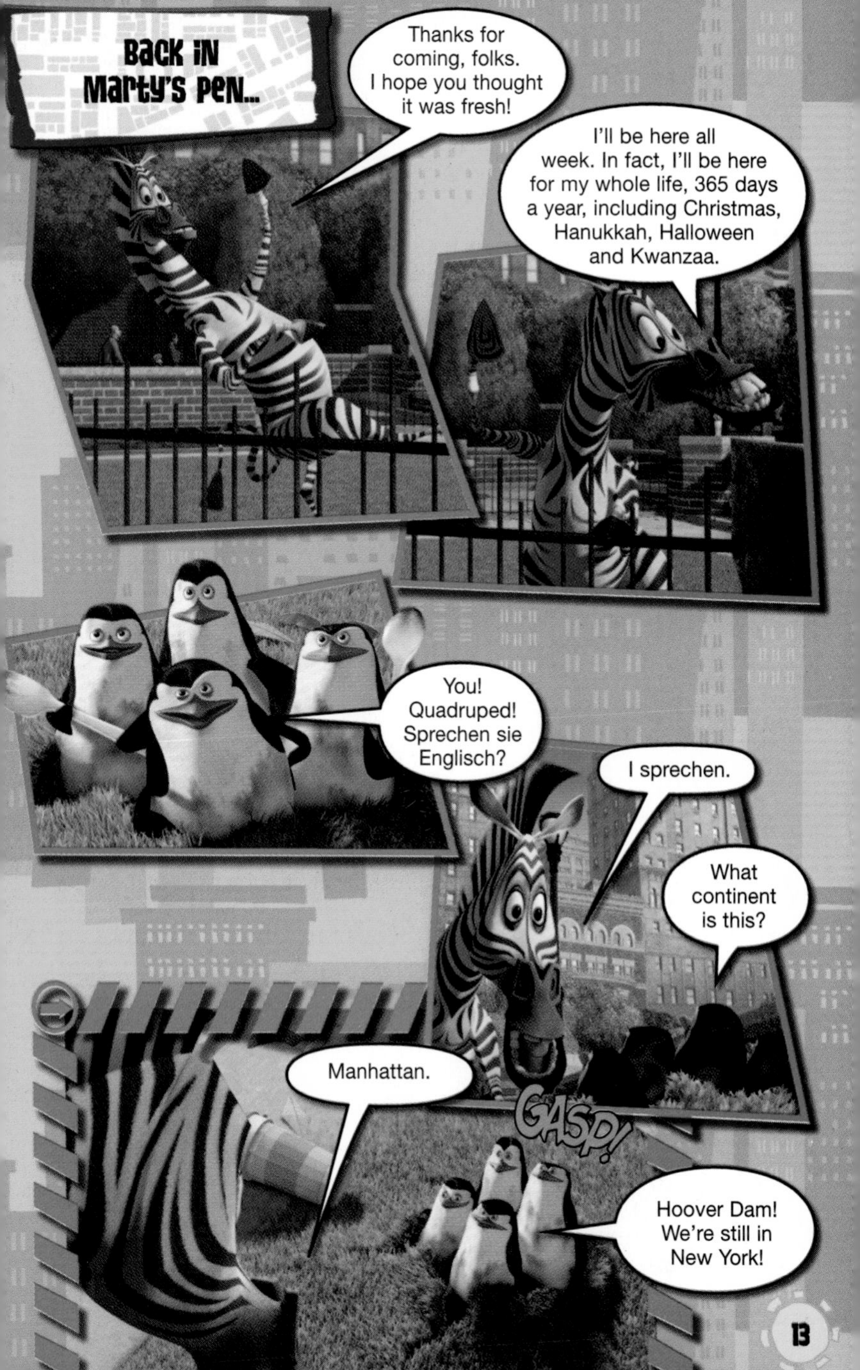
Back in Marty's Pen...
Thanks for coming, folks. I hope you thought it was fresh!
I'll be here all week. In fact, I'll be here for my whole life, 365 days a year, including Christmas, Hanukkah, Halloween and Kwanzaa.
You! Quadruped! Sprechen sie Englisch?
I sprechen.
What continent is this?
Manhattan.
GASP!
Hoover Dam! We're still in New York!

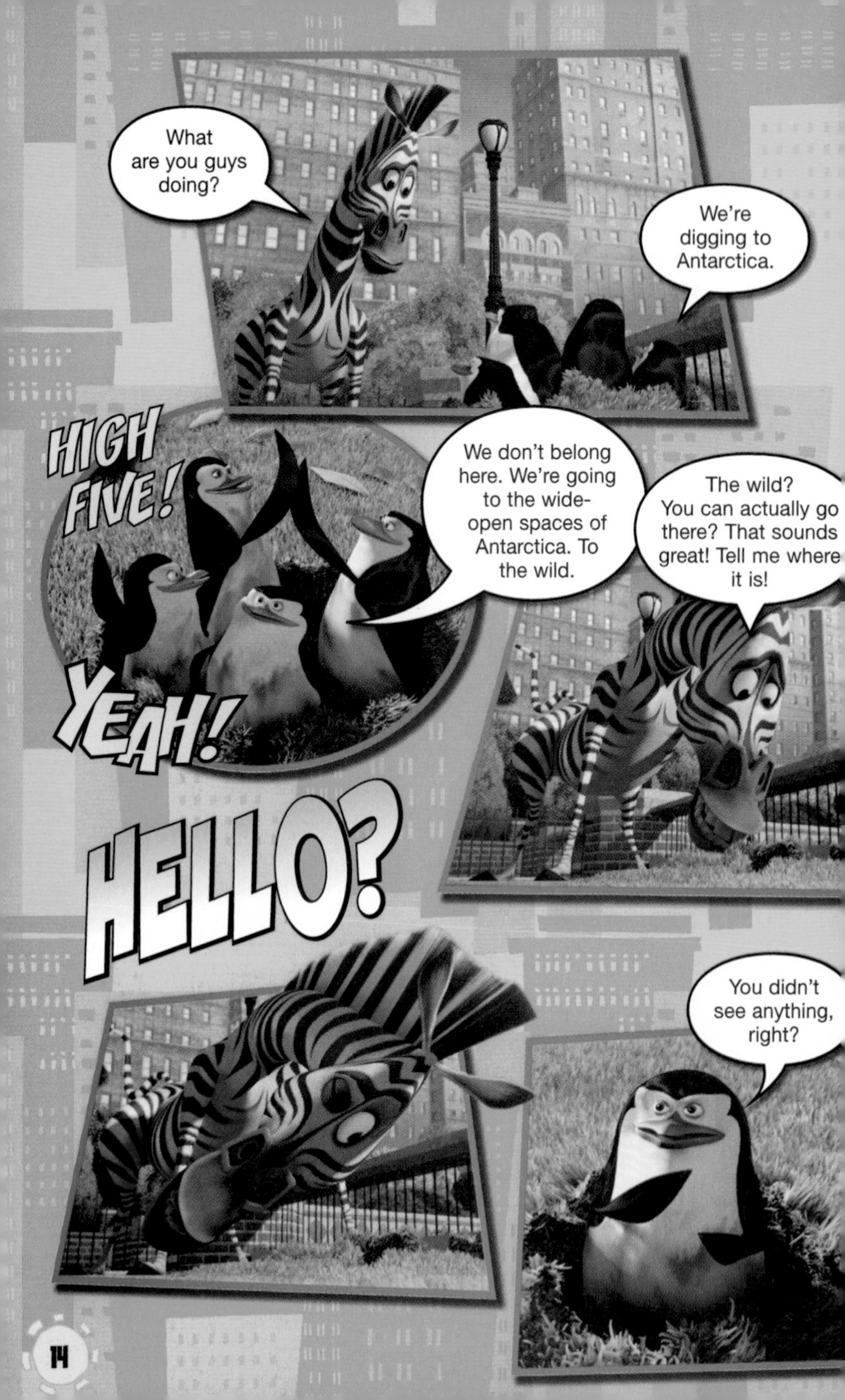
What are you guys doing?
We're digging to Antarctica.
HIGH FIVE!
YEAH!
We don't belong here. We're going to the wide-open spaces of Antarctica. To the wild.
The wild? You can actually go there? That sounds great! Tell me where it is!
HELLO?
You didn't see anything, right?

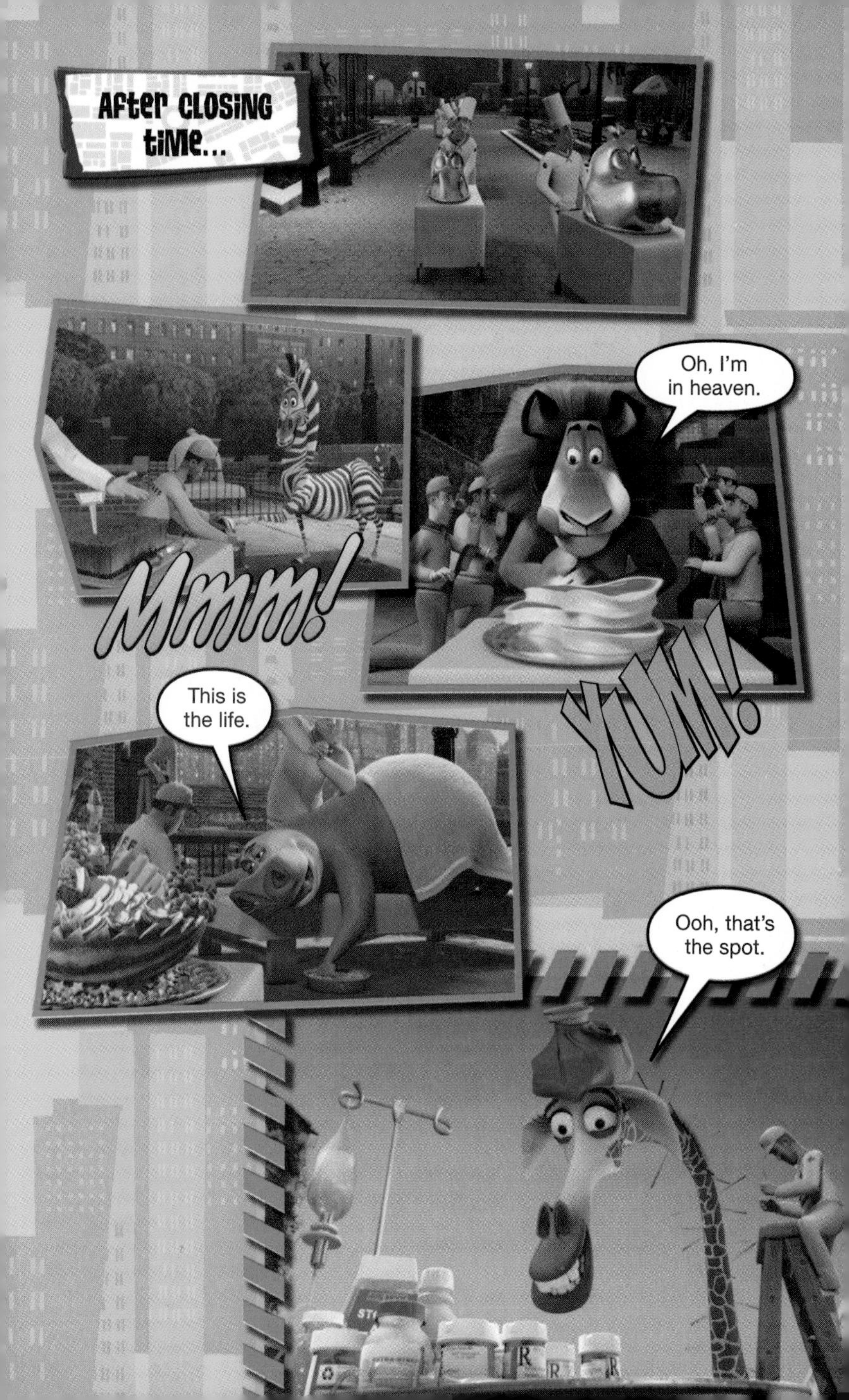
After closing time...
Mmm!
Oh, I'm in heaven.
Yum!
This is the life.
Ooh, that's the spot.

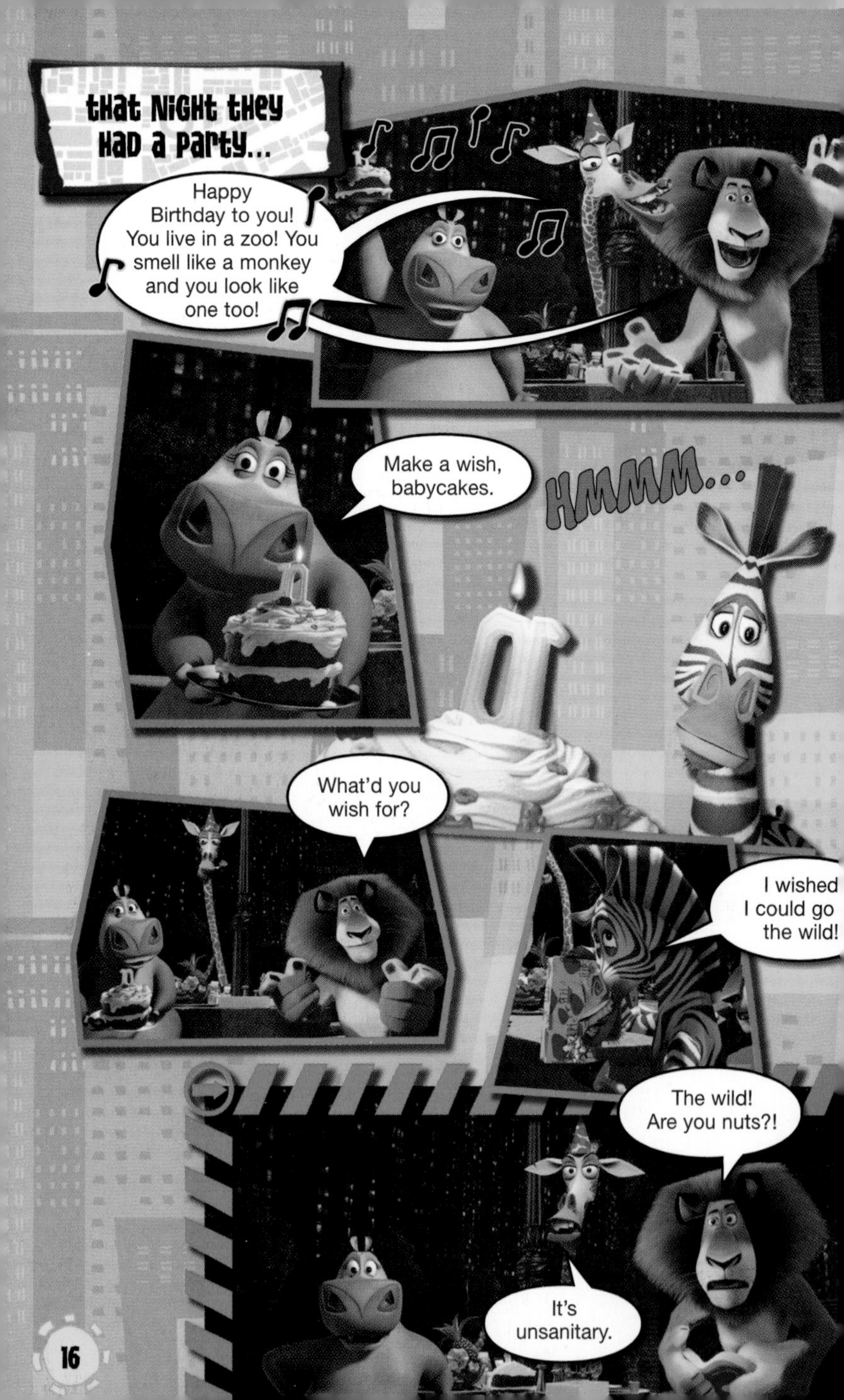
THAT NIGHT THEY HAD A PARTY...
Happy Birthday to you! You live in a zoo! You smell like a monkey and you look like one too!
Make a wish, babycakes.
HMMM...
What'd you wish for?
I wished I could go the wild!
The wild! Are you nuts?!
It's unsanitary.

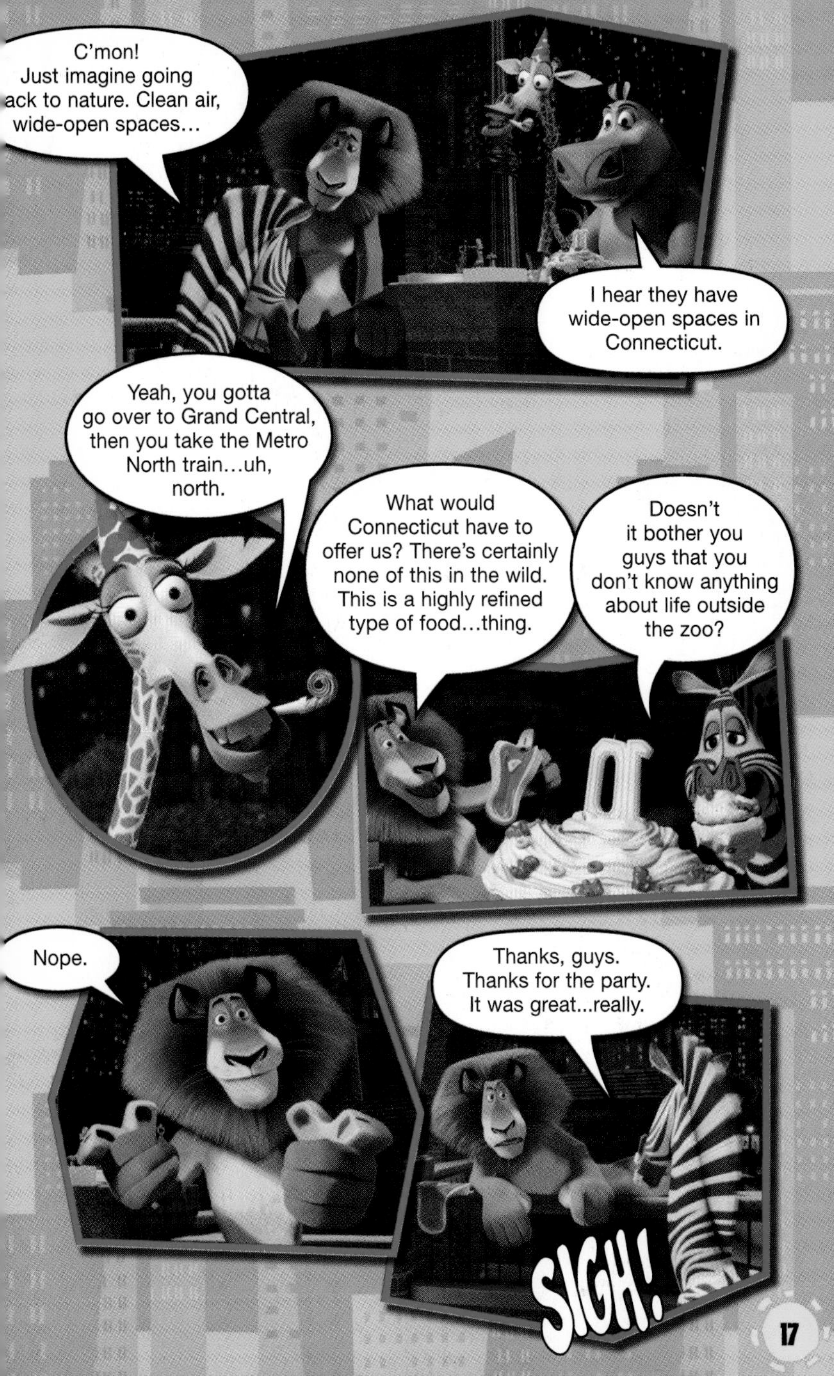
C'mon! Just imagine going ack to nature. Clean air, wide-open spaces…
I hear they have wide-open spaces in Connecticut.
Yeah, you gotta go over to Grand Central, then you take the Metro North train…uh, north.
What would Connecticut have to offer us? There's certainly none of this in the wild. This is a highly refined type of food…thing.
Doesn't it bother you guys that you don't know anything about life outside the zoo?
Nope.
Thanks, guys. Thanks for the party. It was great...really.
SIGH!

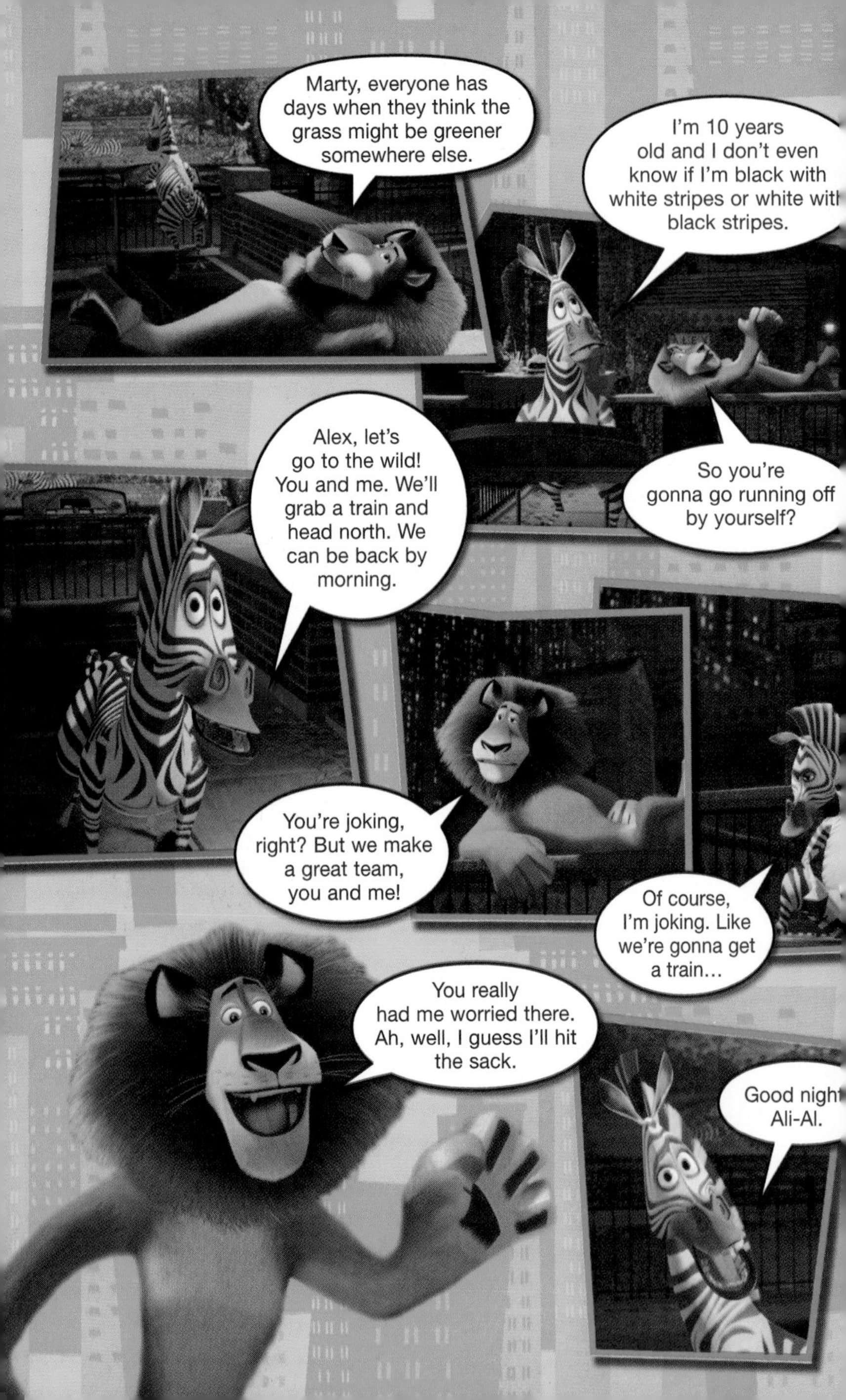
Marty, everyone has days when they think the grass might be greener somewhere else.
I'm 10 years old and I don't even know if I'm black with white stripes or white wit black stripes.
So you're gonna go running off by yourself?
Alex, let's go to the wild! You and me. We'll grab a train and head north. We can be back by morning.
You're joking, right? But we make a great team, you and me!
Of course, I'm joking. Like we're gonna get a train…
You really had me worried there. Ah, well, I guess I'll hit the sack.
Good nigh Ali-Al.

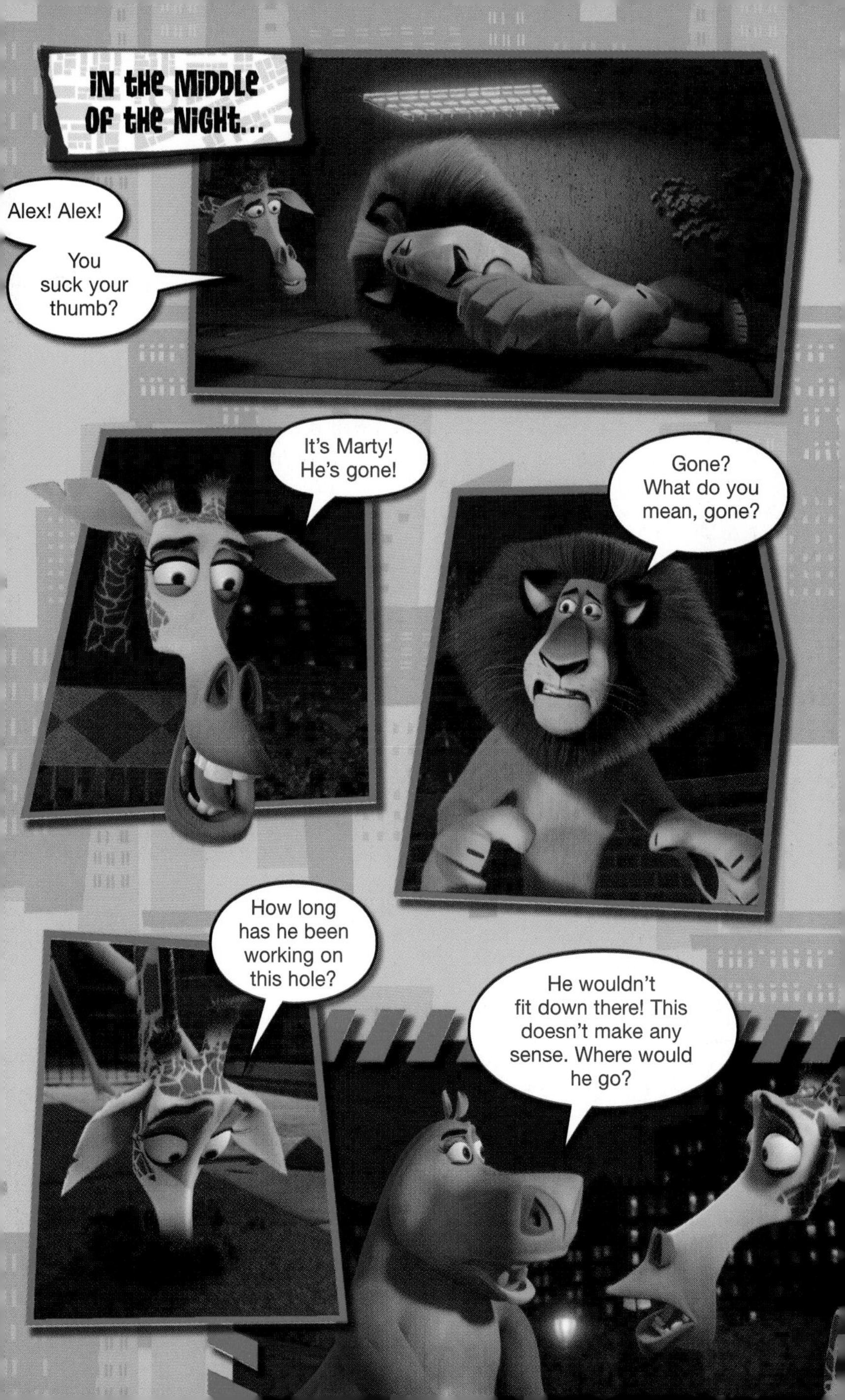
IN THE MIDDLE OF THE NIGHT...
Alex! Alex!
You suck your thumb?
It's Marty! He's gone!
Gone? What do you mean, gone?
How long has he been working on this hole?
He wouldn't fit down there! This doesn't make any sense. Where would he go?

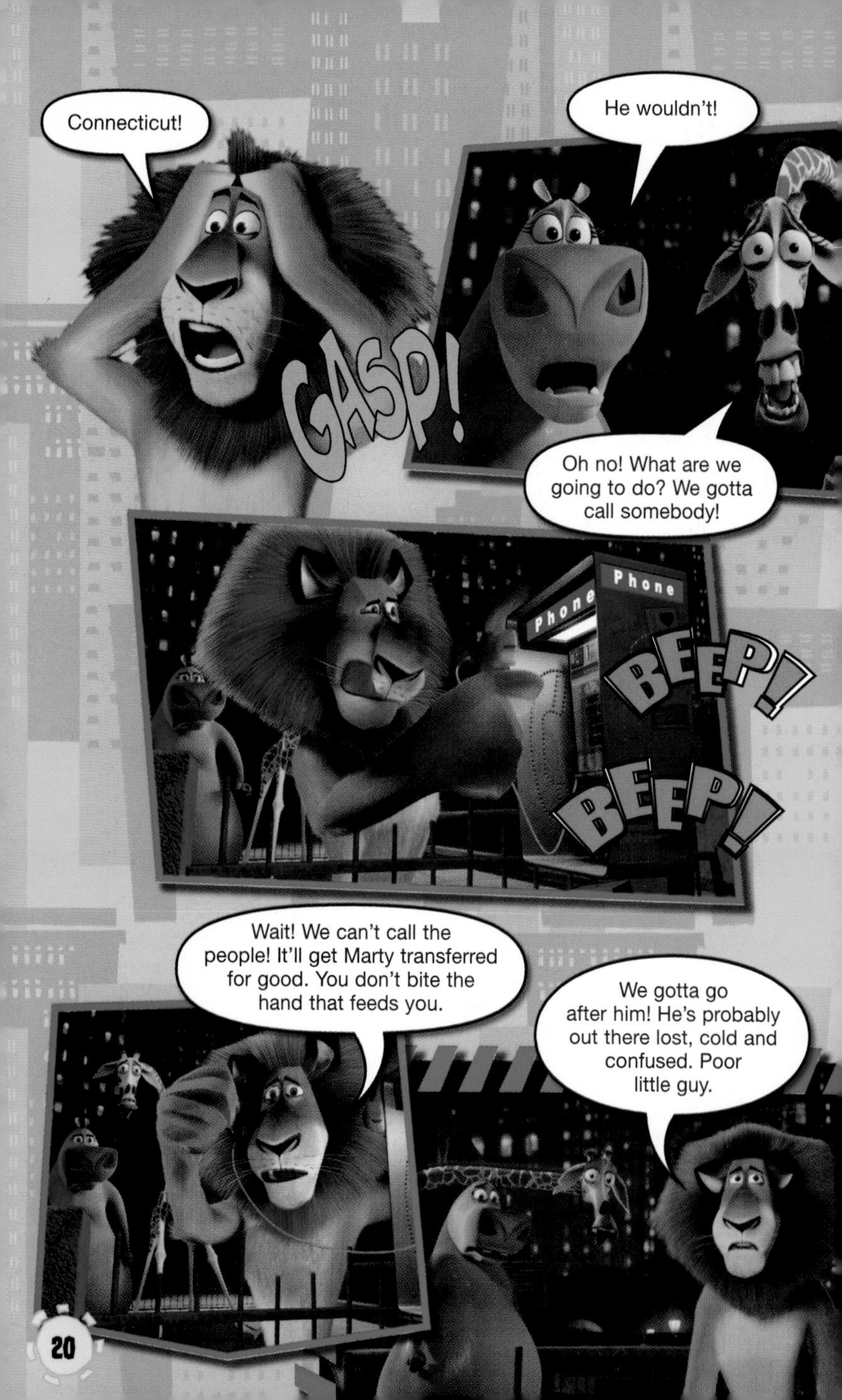
Connecticut!
GASP!
He wouldn't!
Oh no! What are we going to do? We gotta call somebody!
Phone
Phone
BEEP!
BEEP!
Wait! We can't call the people! It'll get Marty transferred for good. You don't bite the hand that feeds you.
We gotta go after him! He's probably out there lost, cold and confused. Poor little guy.

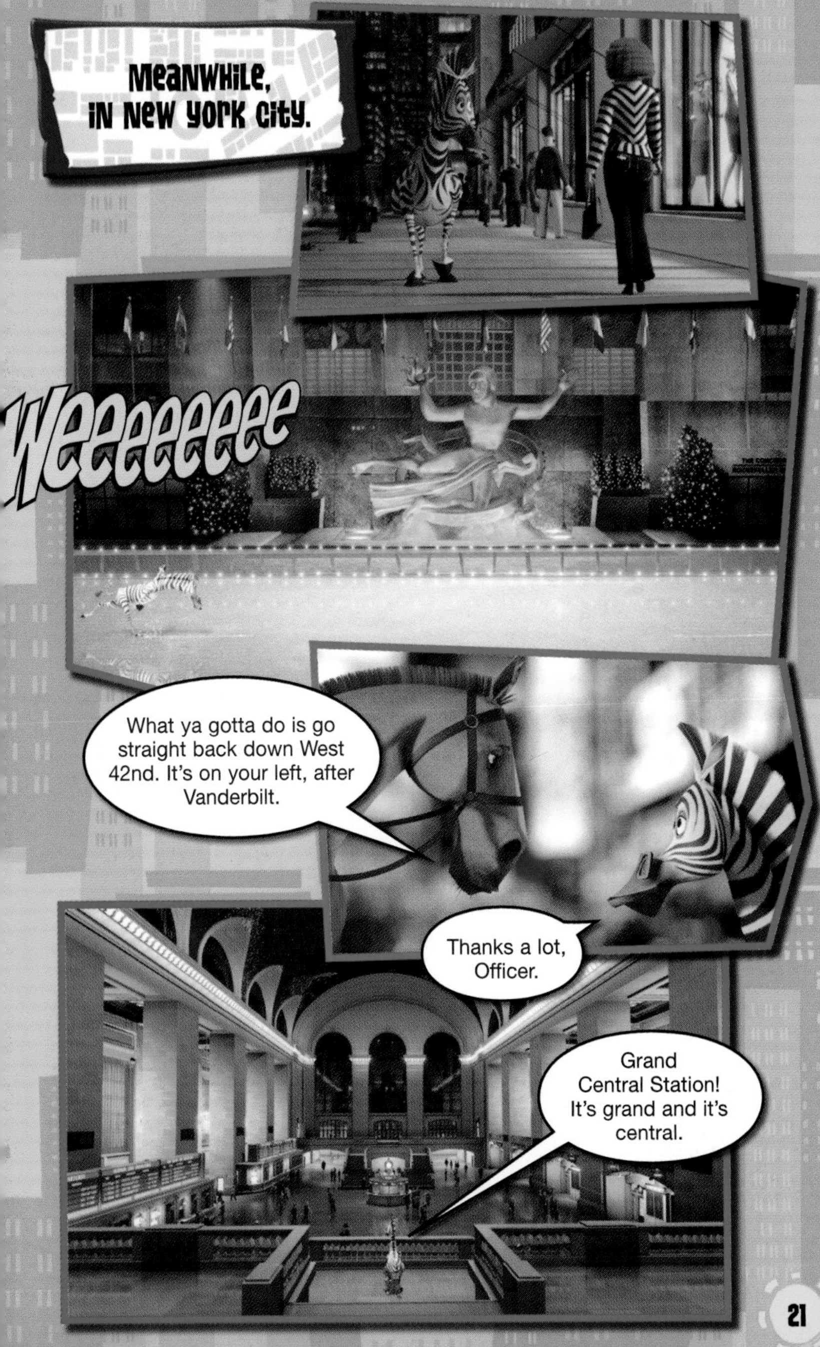
MEANWHILE, IN NEW YORK CITY.
WEEEEEEEE
What ya gotta do is go straight back down West 42nd. It's on your left, after Vanderbilt.
Thanks a lot, Officer.
Grand Central Station! It's grand and it's central.

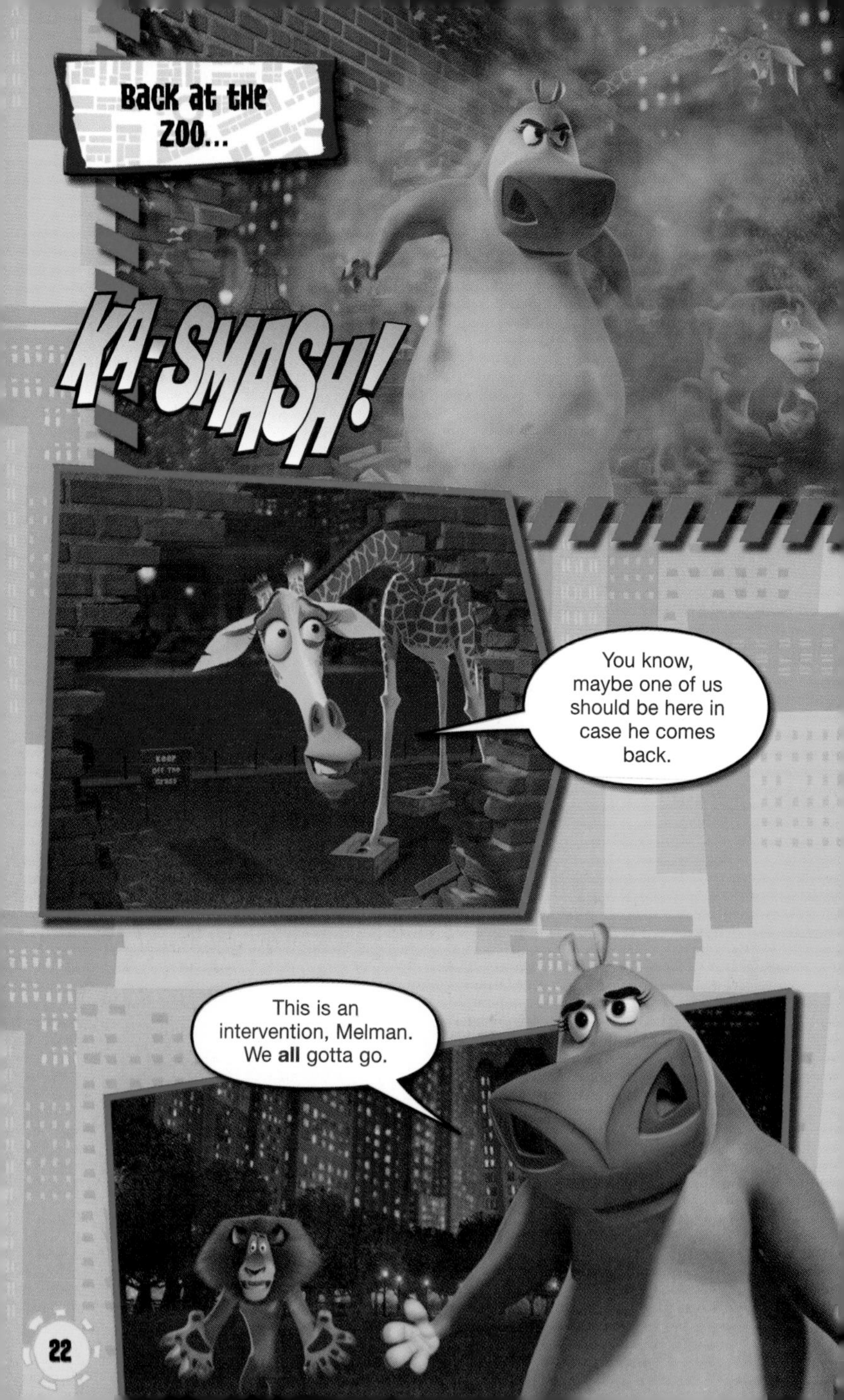
Back at the zoo...
KA-SMASH!
You know, maybe one of us should be here in case he comes back.
This is an intervention, Melman. We **all** gotta go.

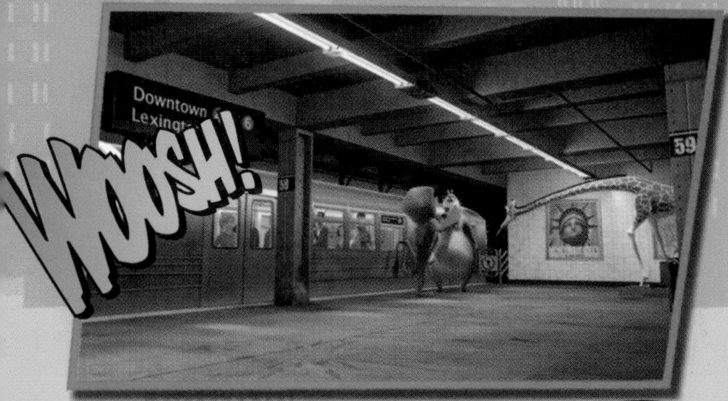

Downtown
WOOSH!

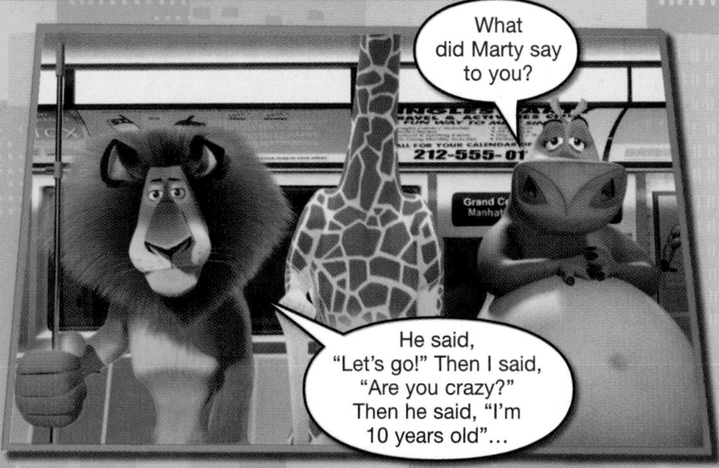

What did Marty say to you?
212-555-01
He said, "Let's go!" Then I said, "Are you crazy?" Then he said, "I'm 10 years old"…

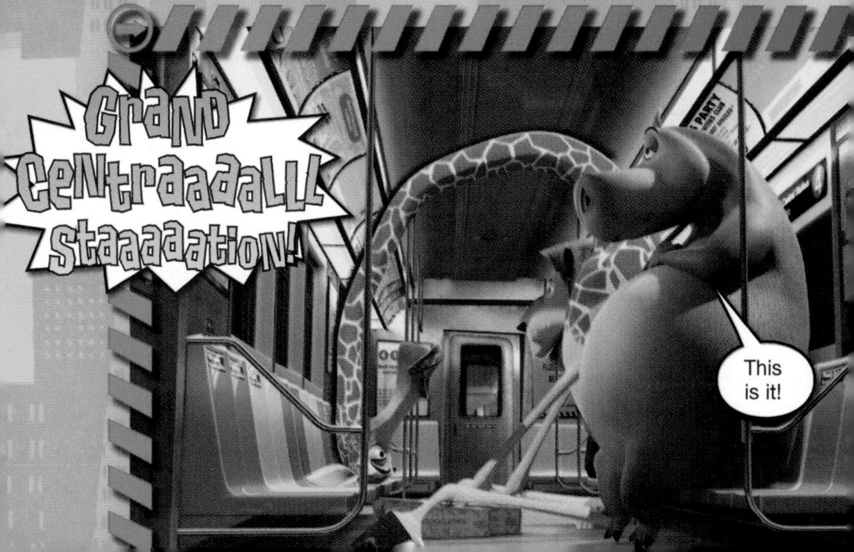

Grand Centraaaaalll Staaaaation!
This is it!

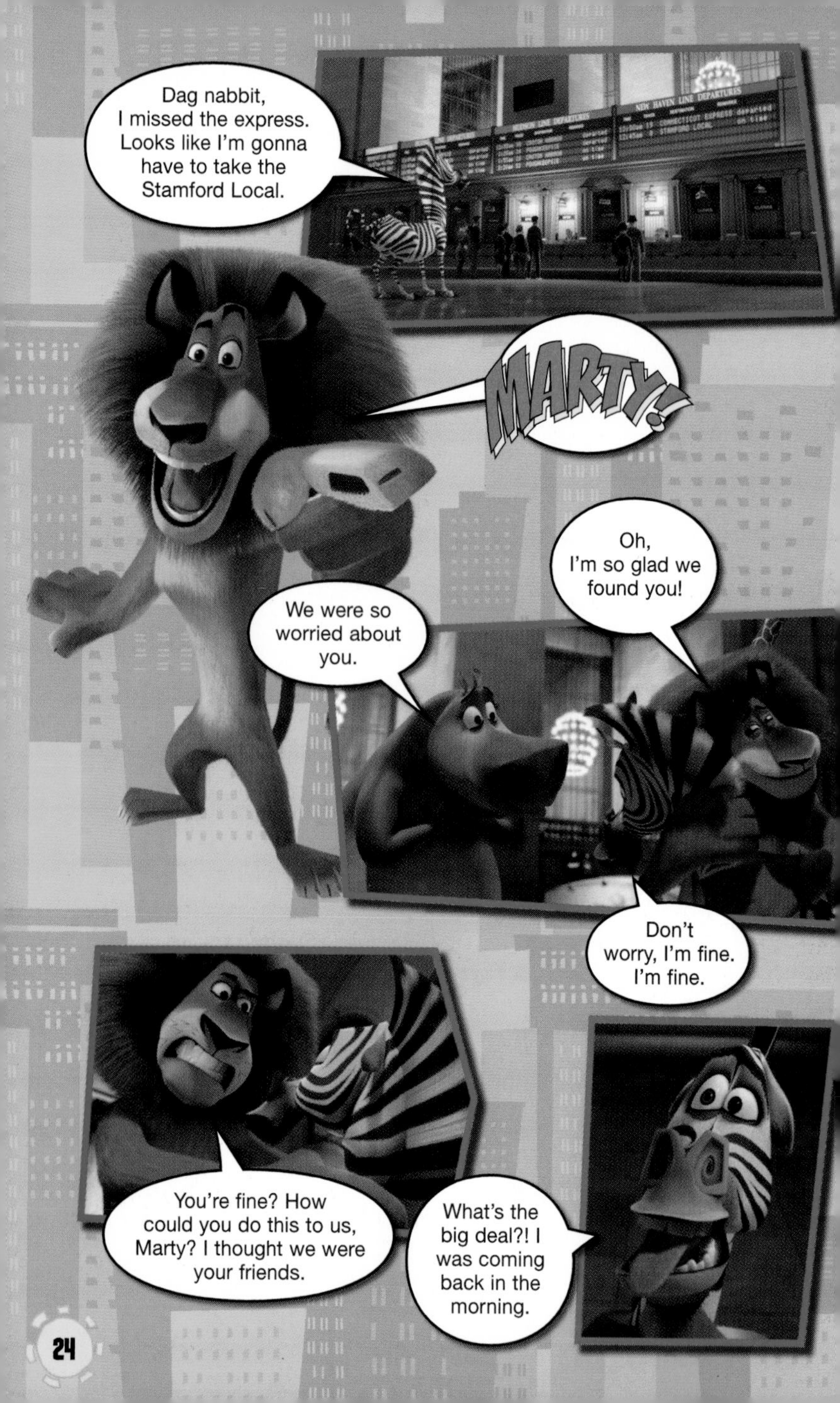

Dag nabbit, I missed the express. Looks like I'm gonna have to take the Stamford Local.
NEW HAVEN LINE DEPARTURES
MARTY!
We were so worried about you.
Oh, I'm so glad we found you!
Don't worry, I'm fine. I'm fine.
You're fine? How could you do this to us, Marty? I thought we were your friends.
What's the big deal?! I was coming back in the morning.

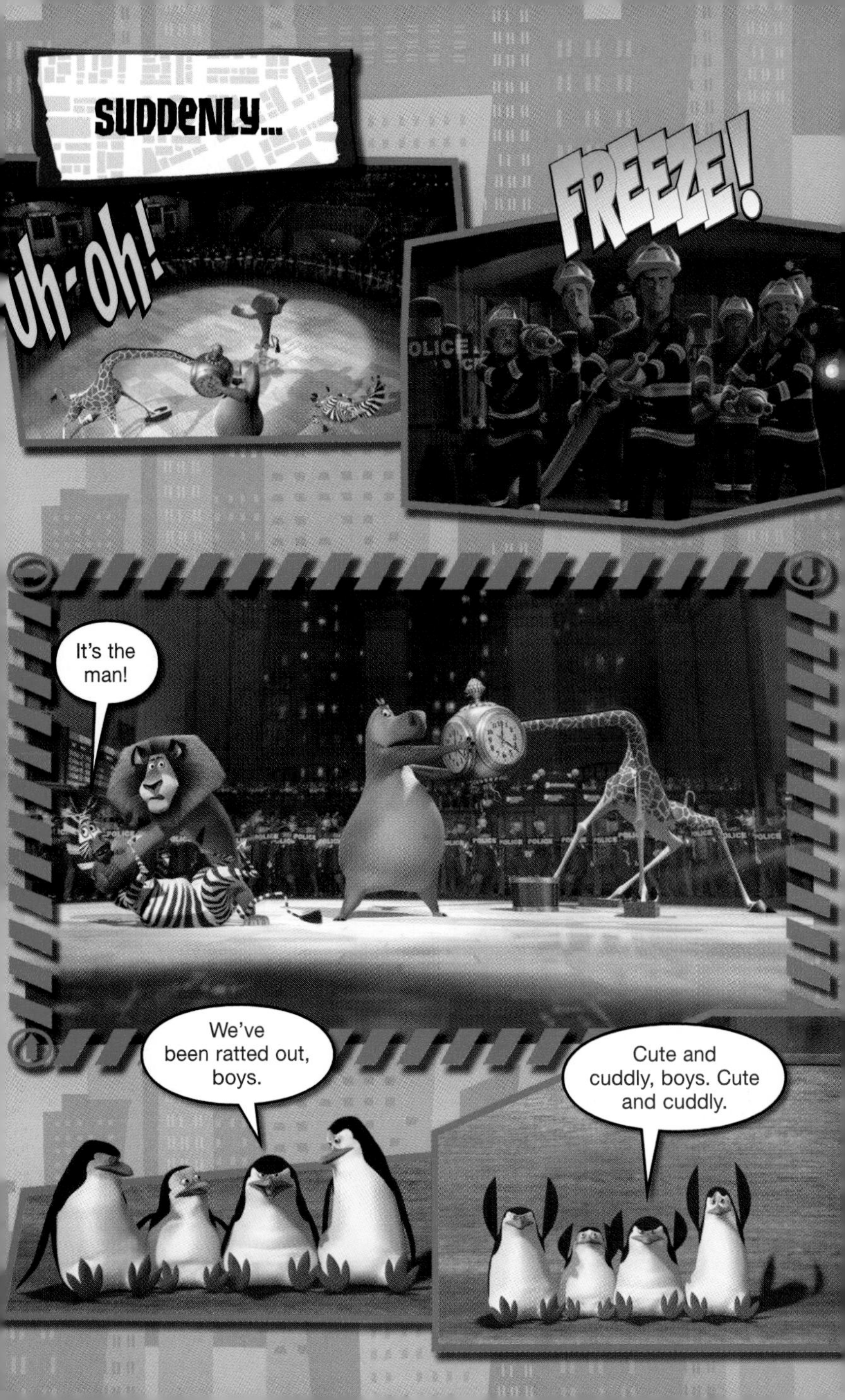
SUDDENLY...
Uh-oh!
FREEZE!
It's the man!
We've been ratted out, boys.
Cute and cuddly, boys. Cute and cuddly.

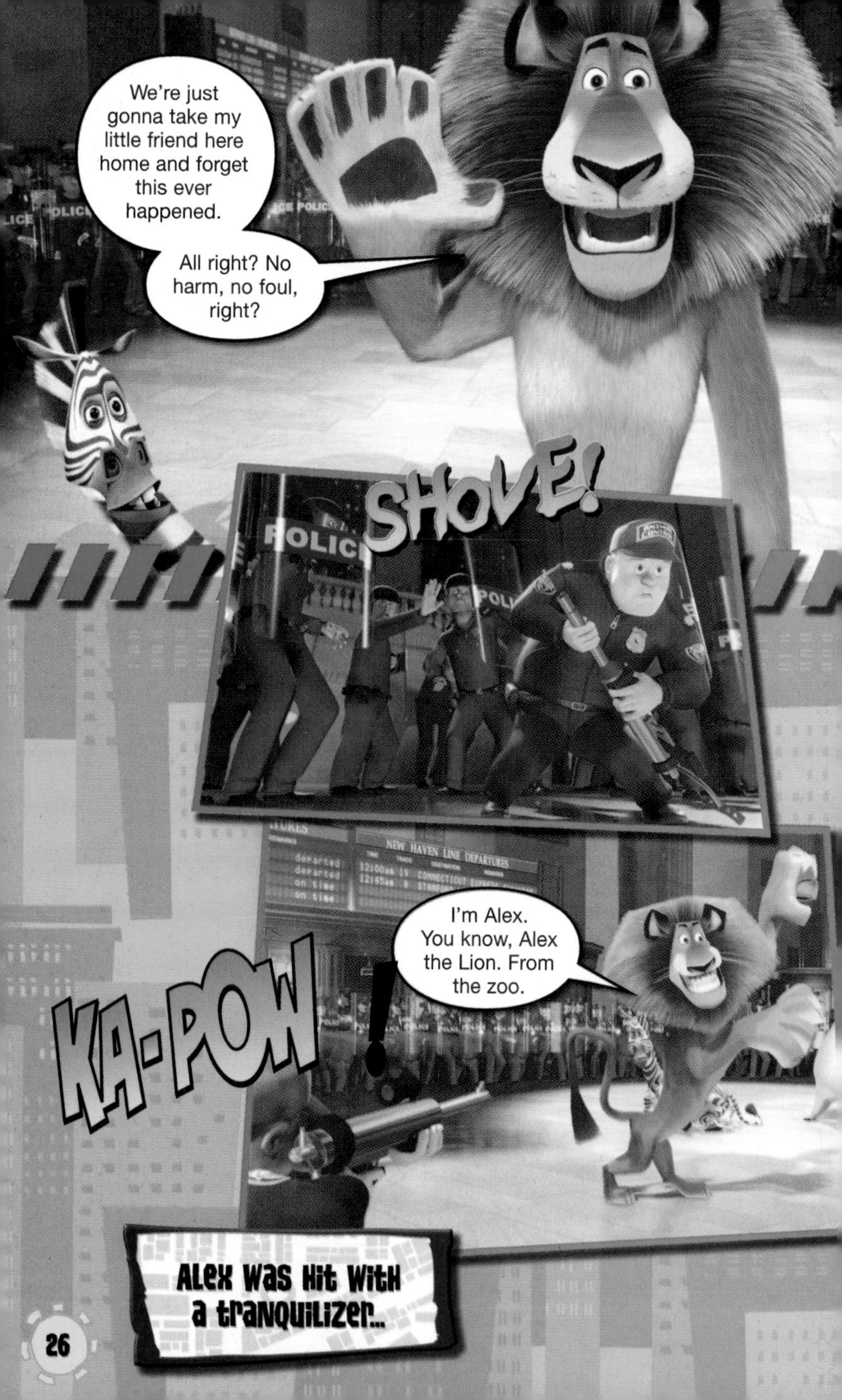
We're just gonna take my little friend here home and forget this ever happened.
All right? No harm, no foul, right?
SHOVE!
POLICE
NEW HAVEN LINE DEPARTURES
I'm Alex. You know, Alex the Lion. From the zoo.
KA-POW!
Alex was hit with a tranquilizer...

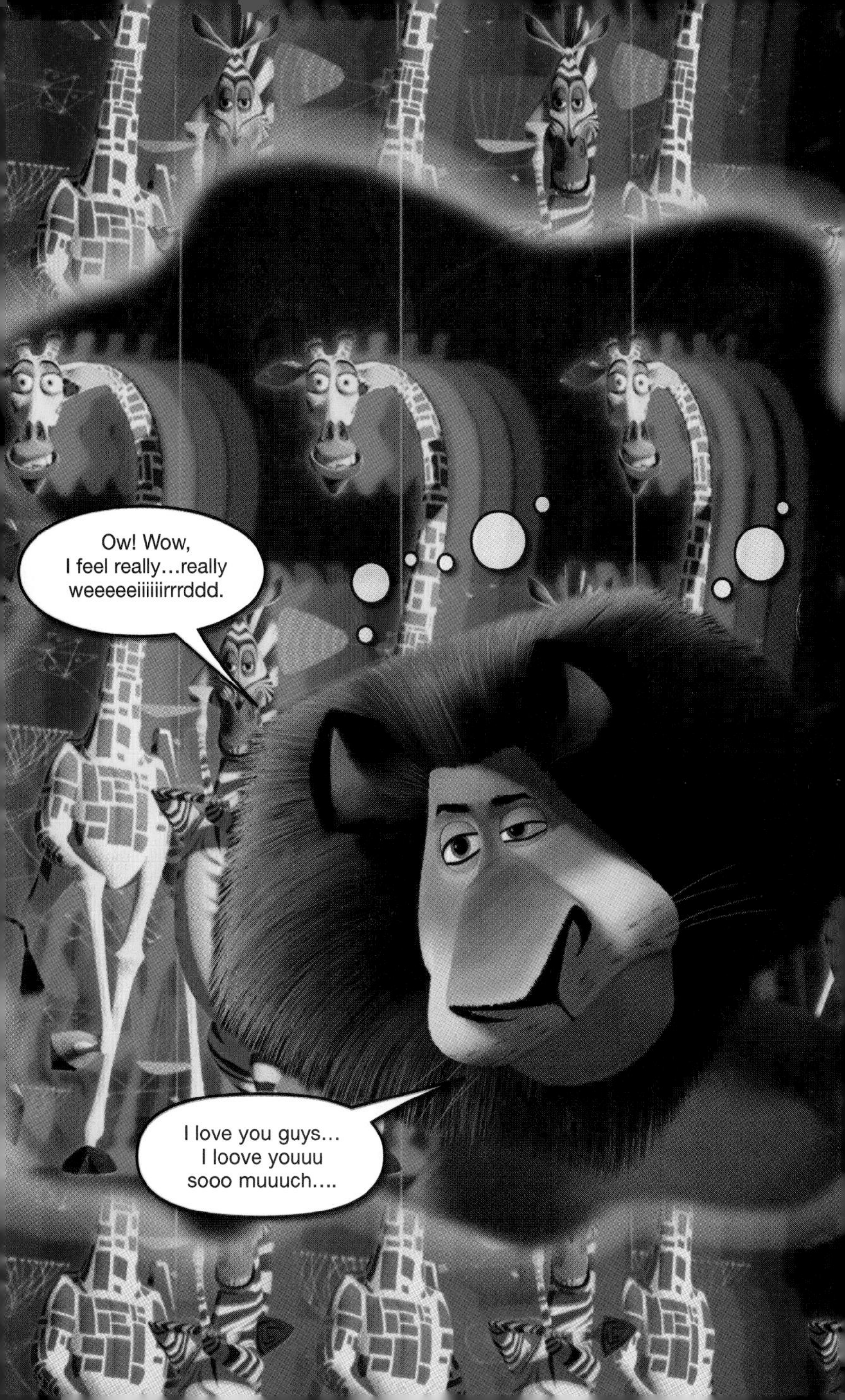
Ow! Wow, I feel really…really weeeeeiiiiiirrrddd.
I love you guys… I loove youuu sooo muuuch….

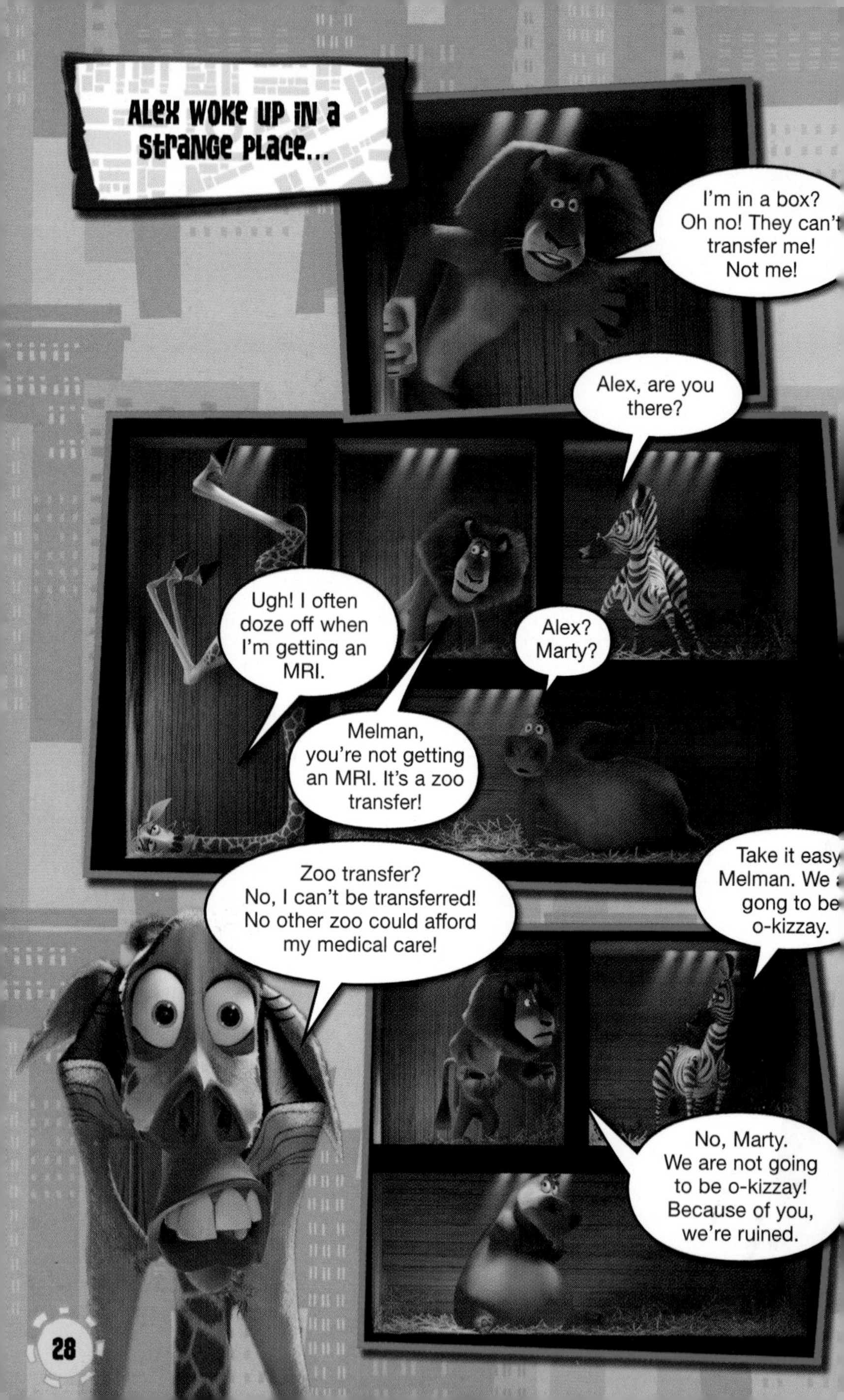

ALEX WOKE UP IN A STRANGE PLACE...
I'm in a box? Oh no! They can't transfer me! Not me!
Alex, are you there?
Ugh! I often doze off when I'm getting an MRI.
Alex? Marty?
Melman, you're not getting an MRI. It's a zoo transfer!
Zoo transfer? No, I can't be transferred! No other zoo could afford my medical care!
Take it easy Melman. We gong to be o-kizzay.
No, Marty. We are not going to be o-kizzay! Because of you, we're ruined.

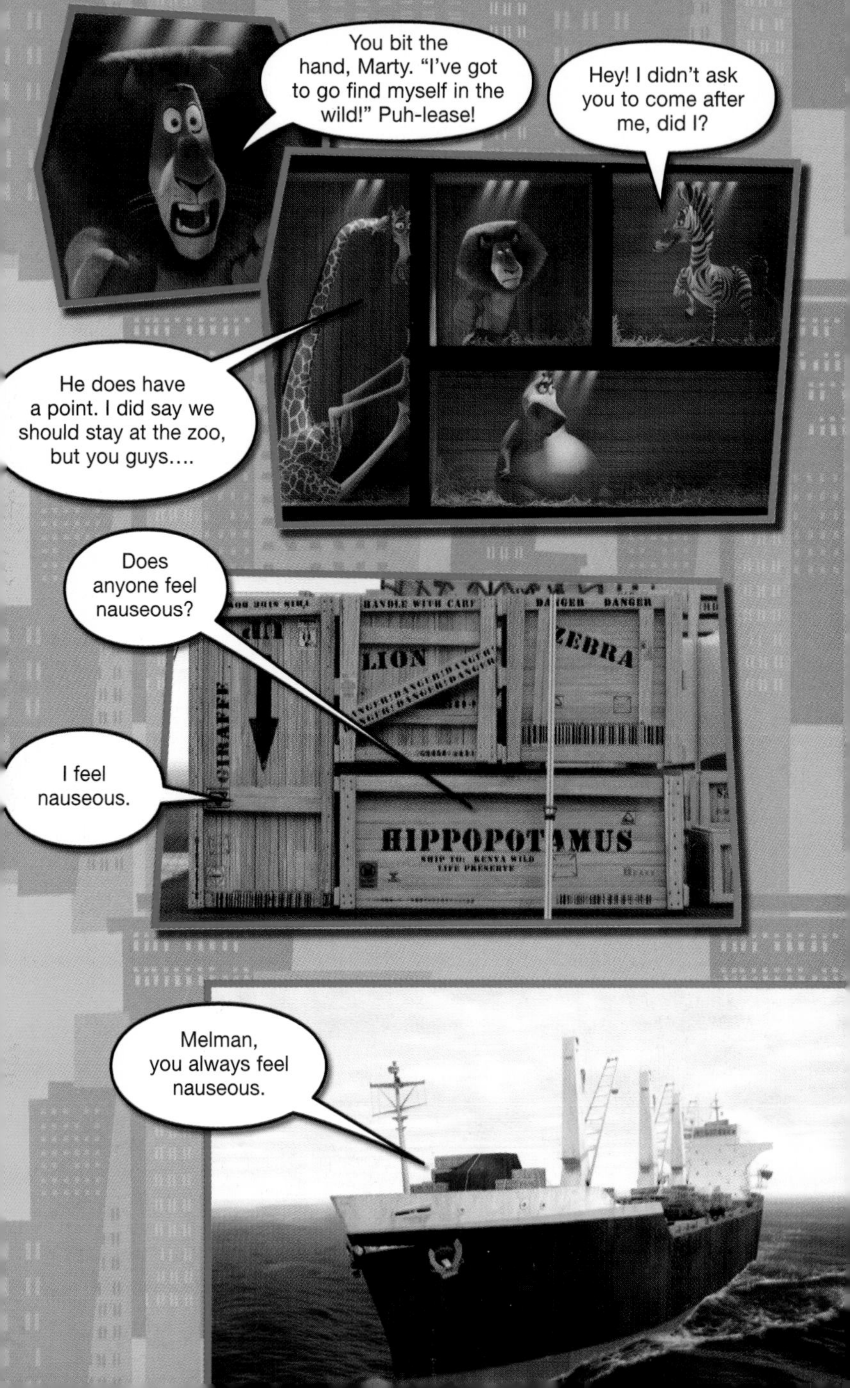
You bit the hand, Marty. "I've got to go find myself in the wild!" Puh-lease!
Hey! I didn't ask you to come after me, did I?
He does have a point. I did say we should stay at the zoo, but you guys....
Does anyone feel nauseous?
LION
ZEBRA
I feel nauseous.
Melman, you always feel nauseous.

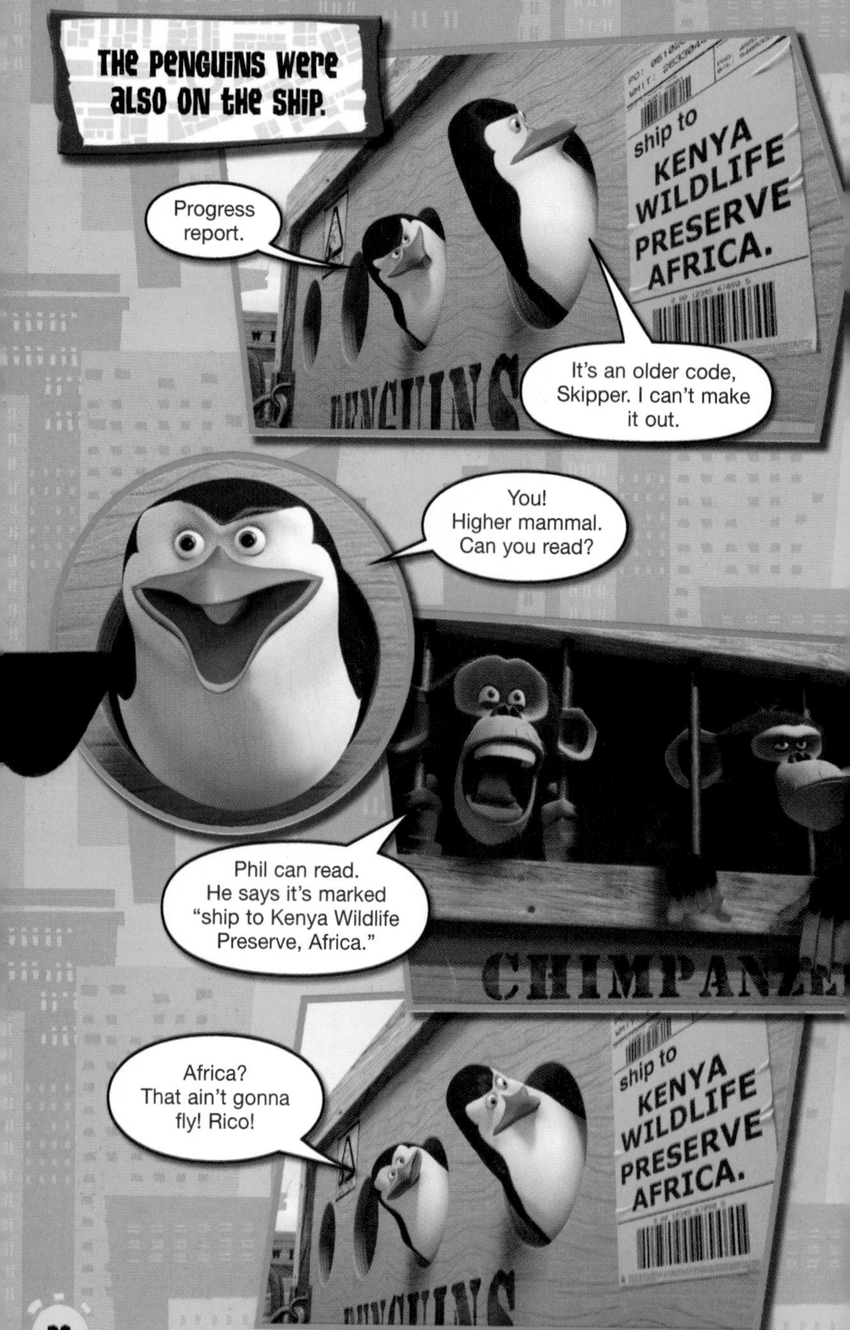
The penguins were also on the ship.
Progress report.
ship to KENYA WILDLIFE PRESERVE AFRICA.
It's an older code, Skipper. I can't make it out.
You! Higher mammal. Can you read?
Phil can read. He says it's marked "ship to Kenya Wildlife Preserve, Africa."
Africa? That ain't gonna fly! Rico!

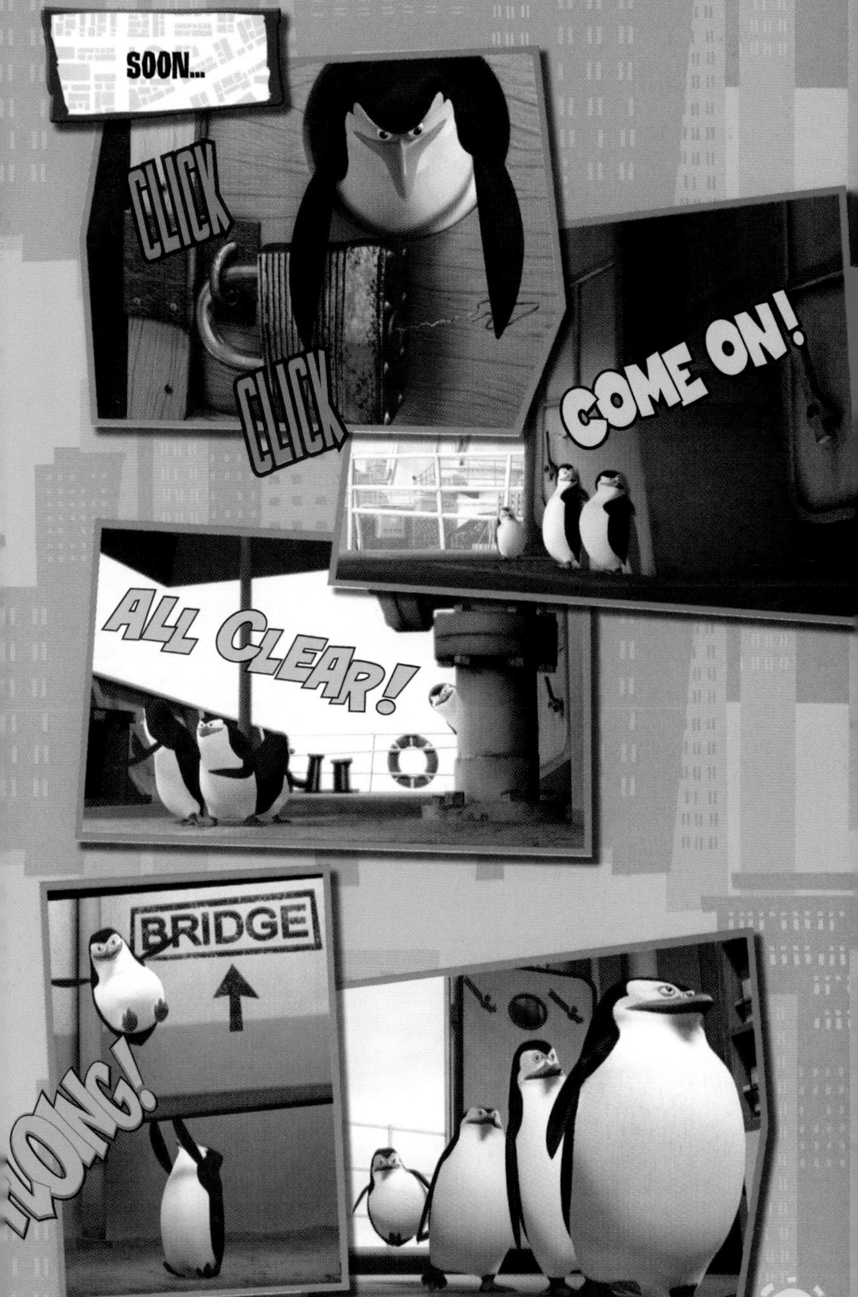

SOON...
CLICK
CLICK
COME ON!
ALL CLEAR!
BRIDGE

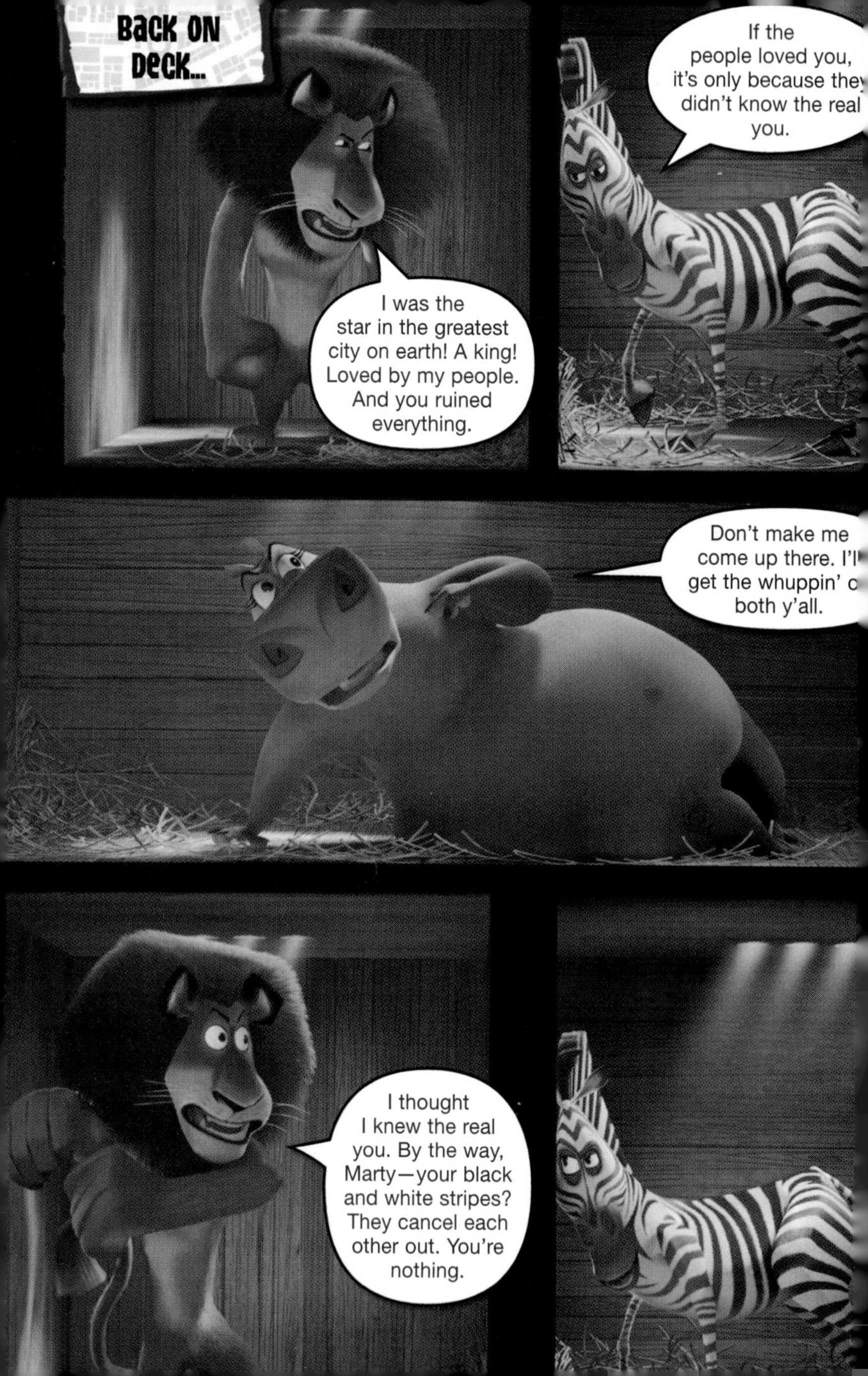
Back on deck...
I was the star in the greatest city on earth! A king! Loved by my people. And you ruined everything.
If the people loved you, it's only because the didn't know the real you.
Don't make me come up there. I'l get the whuppin' o both y'all.
I thought I knew the real you. By the way, Marty—your black and white stripes? They cancel each other out. You're nothing.

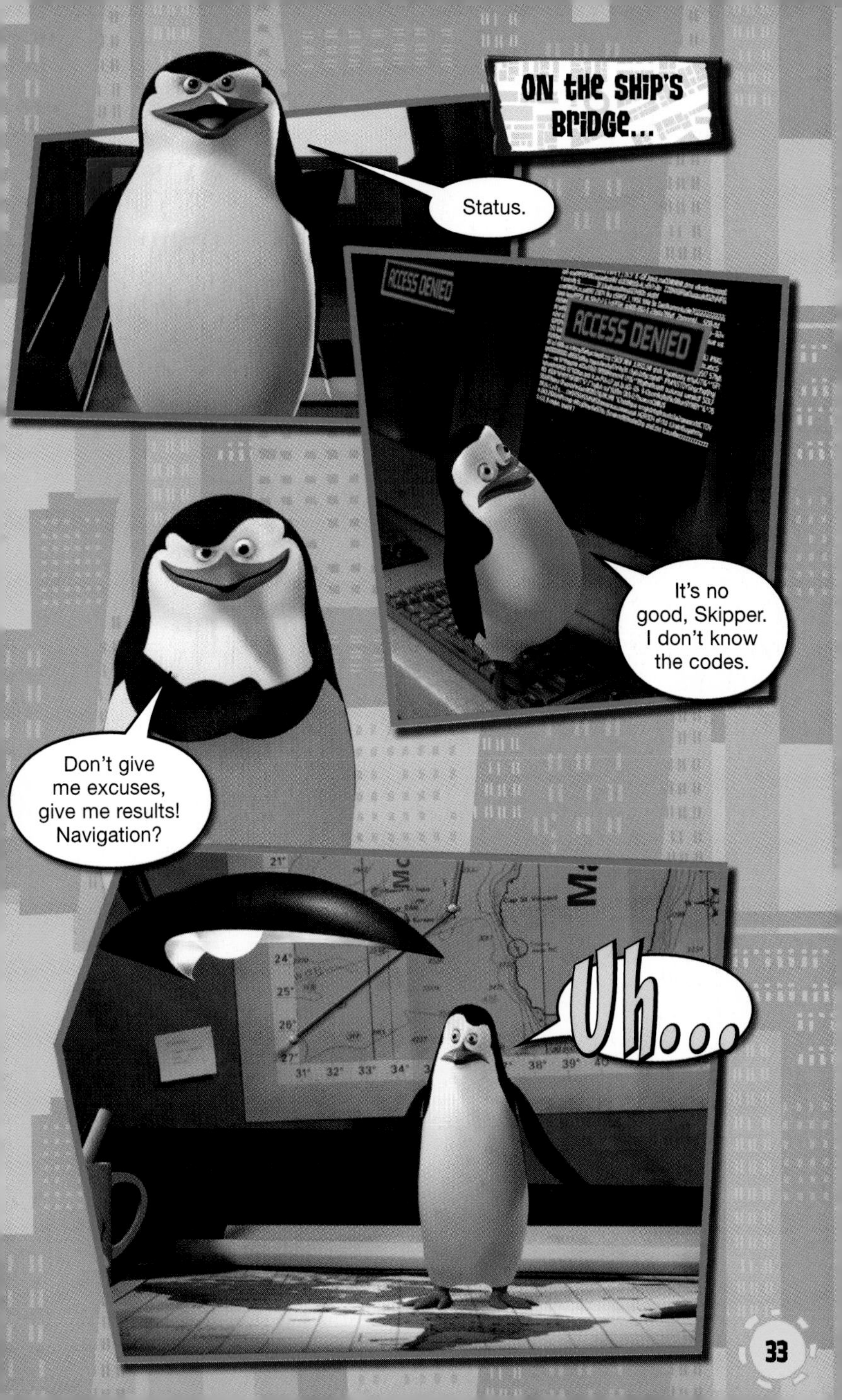
ON THE SHIP'S BRIDGE...
Status.
ACCESS DENIED
ACCESS DENIED
It's no good, Skipper. I don't know the codes.
Don't give me excuses, give me results! Navigation?
Uh...

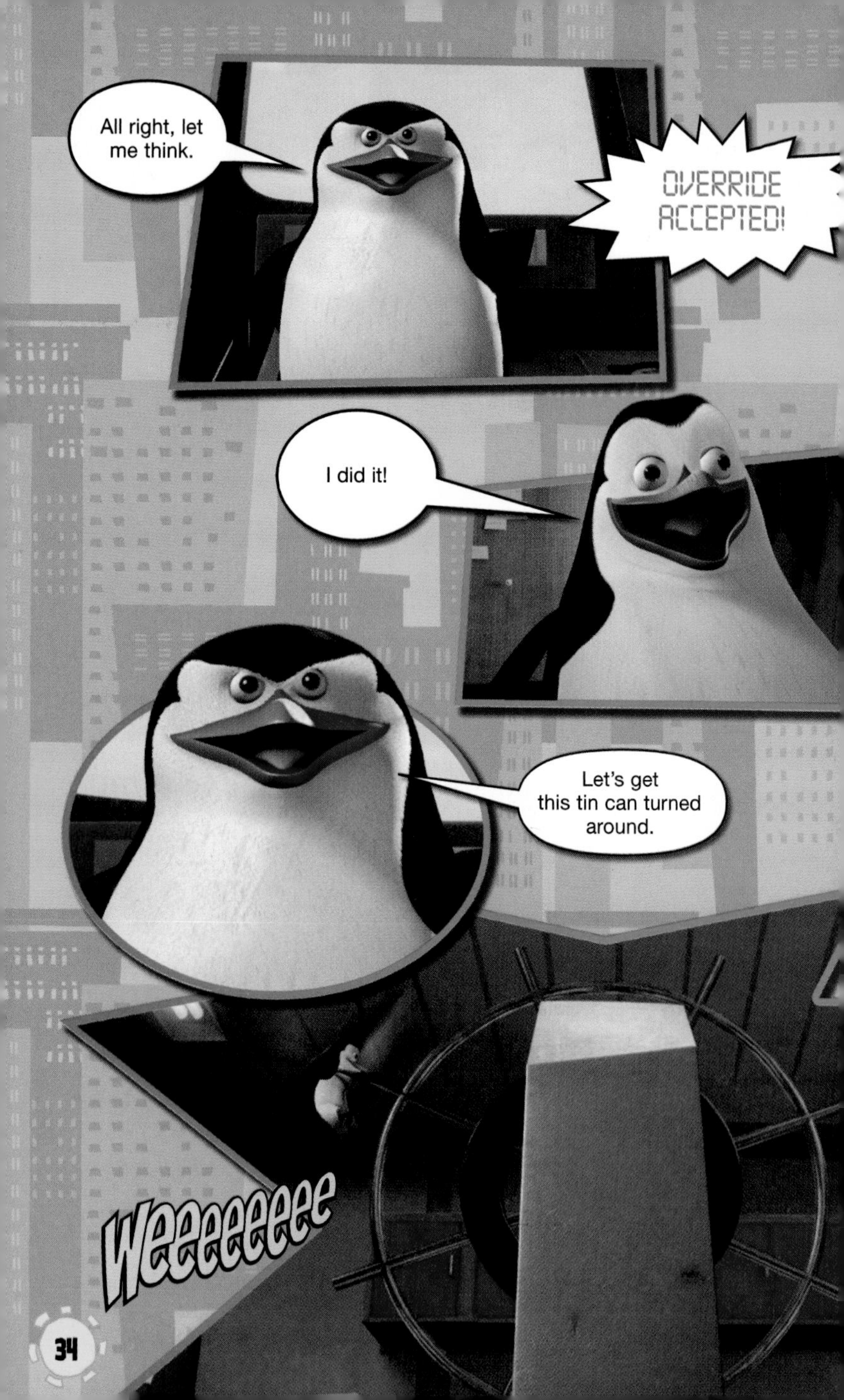
All right, let me think.
OVERRIDE ACCEPTED!
I did it!
Let's get this tin can turned around.
Weeeeeeee

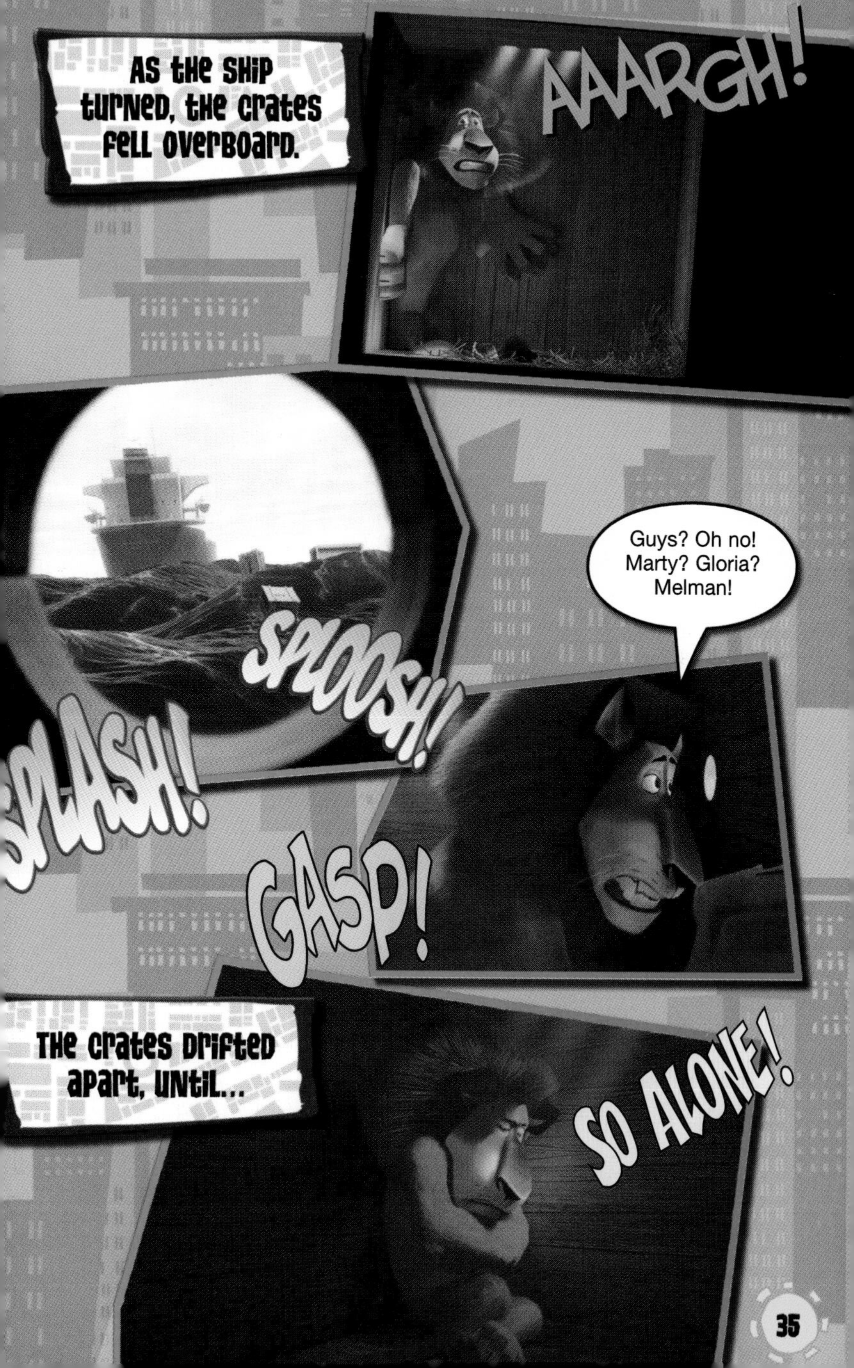

AS THE SHIP TURNED, THE CRATES FELL OVERBOARD.
AAARGH!
SPLOOSH!
SPLASH!
Guys? Oh no! Marty? Gloria? Melman!
GASP!
THE CRATES DRIFTED APART, UNTIL...
SO ALONE!

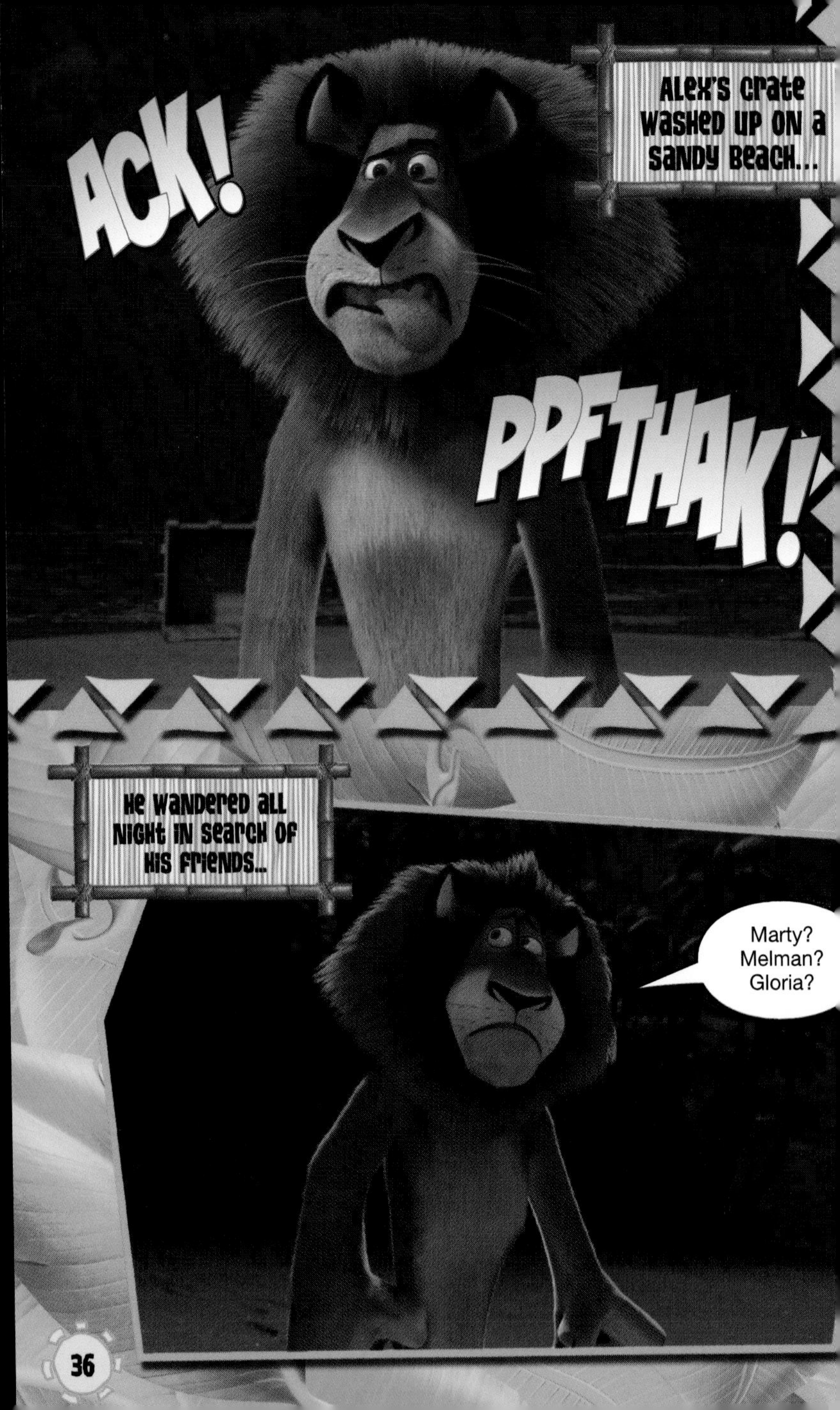
Alex's crate washed up on a sandy beach...
ACK!
PPFTHAK!
He wandered all night in search of his friends...
Marty? Melman? Gloria?

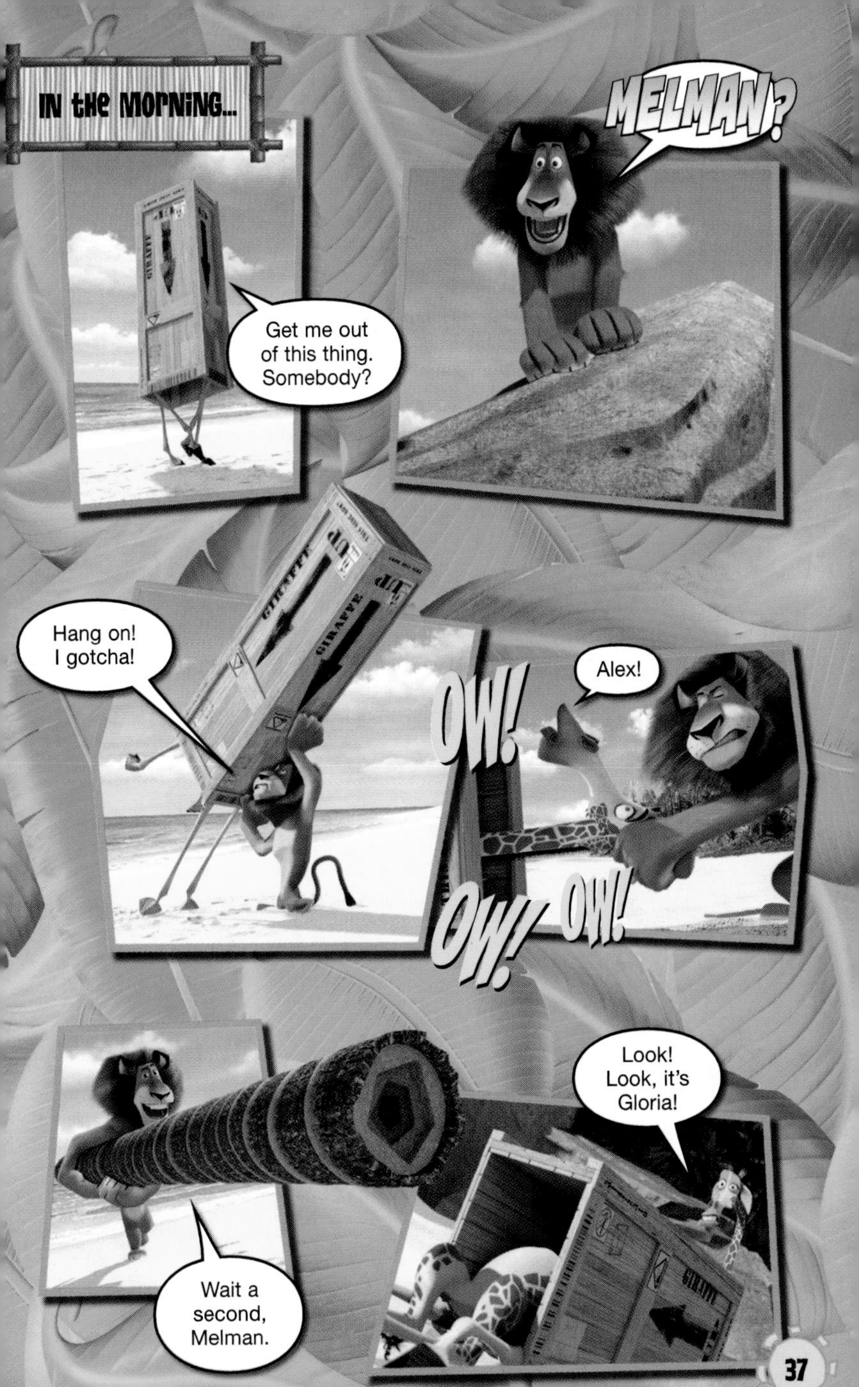
IN THE MORNING...
Get me out of this thing. Somebody?
MELMAN!?
Hang on! I gotcha!
OW!
Alex!
OW!
OW!
Wait a second, Melman.
Look! Look, it's Gloria!

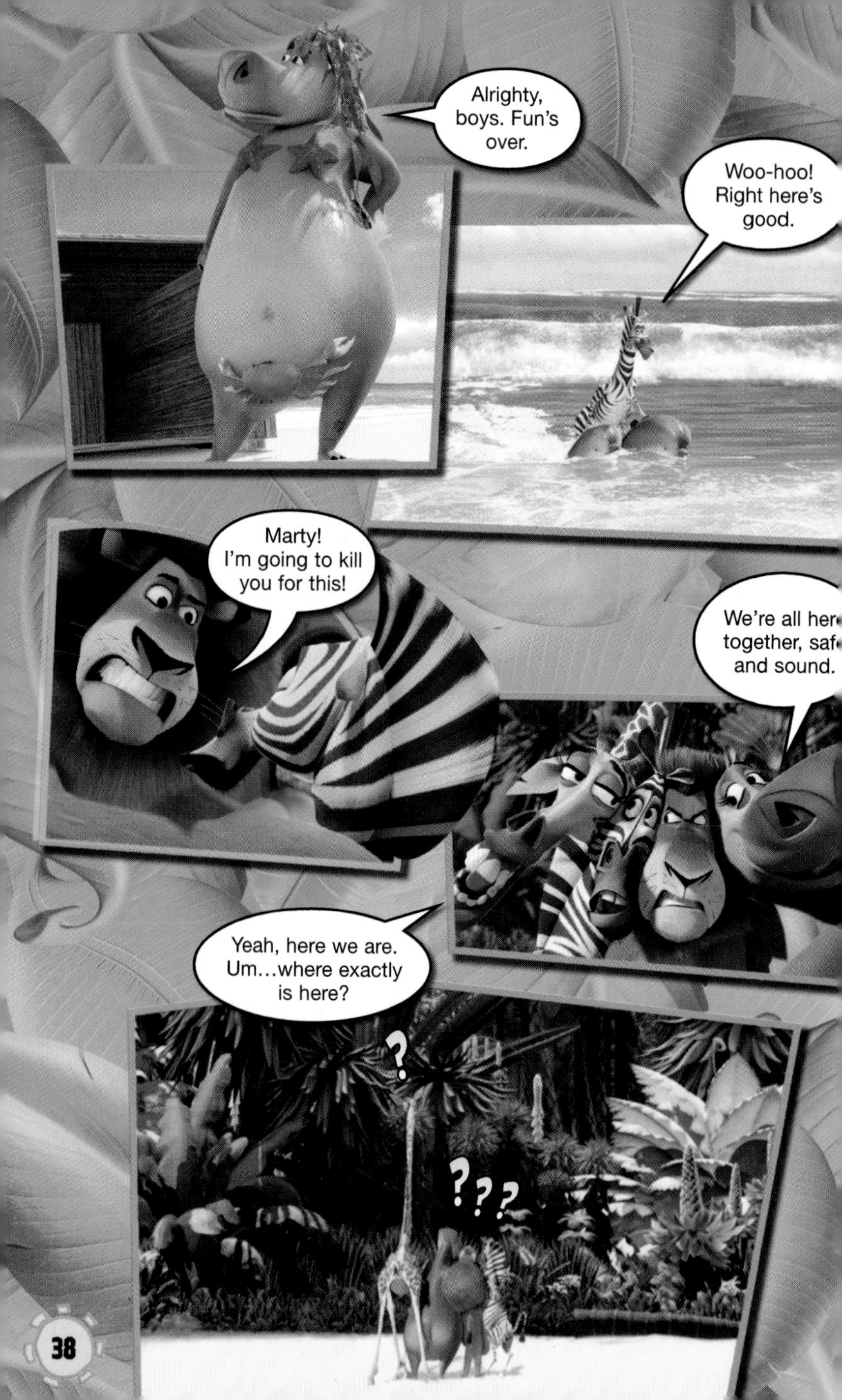

Alrighty, boys. Fun's over.
Woo-hoo! Right here's good.
Marty! I'm going to kill you for this!
We're all here together, safe and sound.
Yeah, here we are. Um…where exactly is here?
?
???

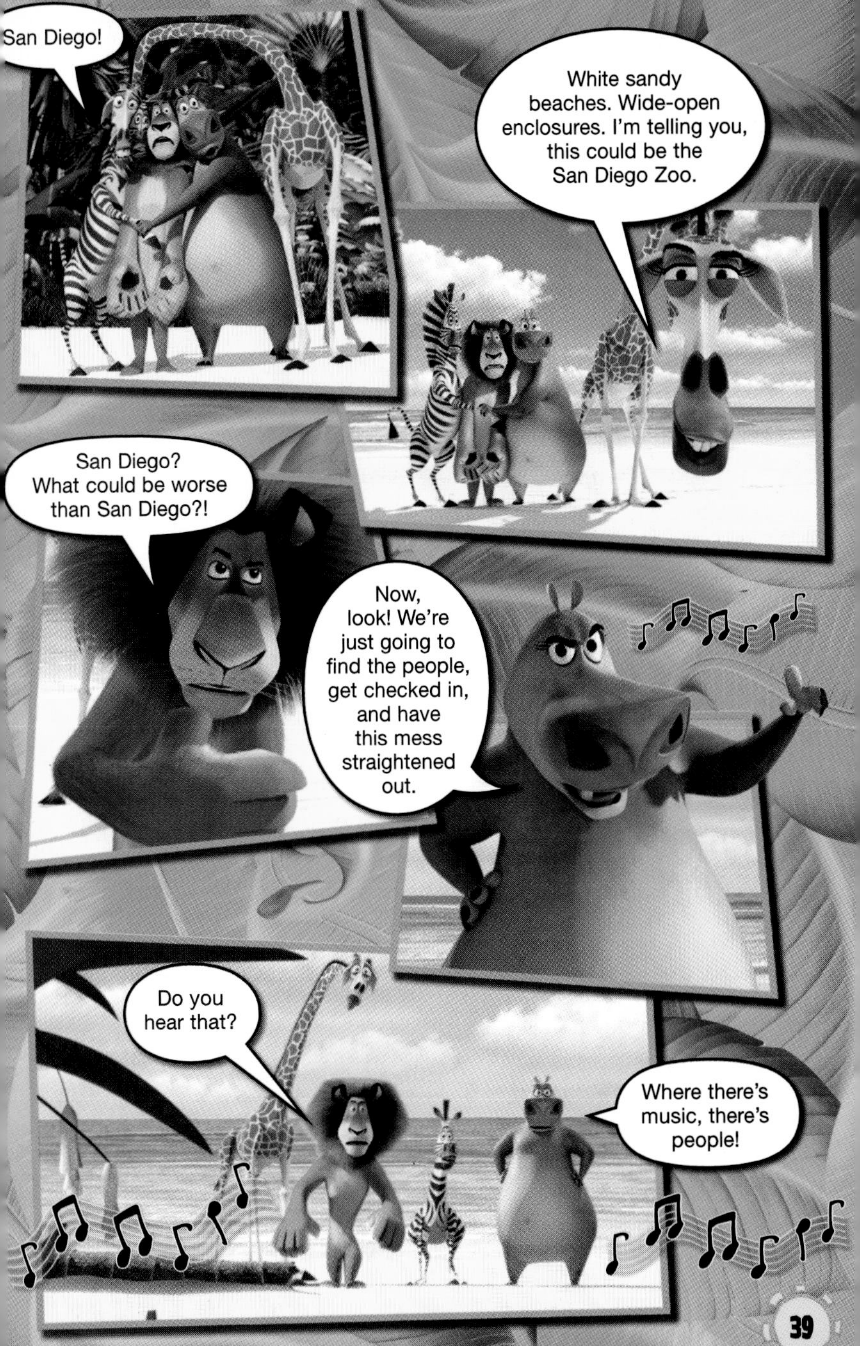
San Diego!
White sandy beaches. Wide-open enclosures. I'm telling you, this could be the San Diego Zoo.
San Diego? What could be worse than San Diego?!
Now, look! We're just going to find the people, get checked in, and have this mess straightened out.
Do you hear that?
Where there's music, there's people!

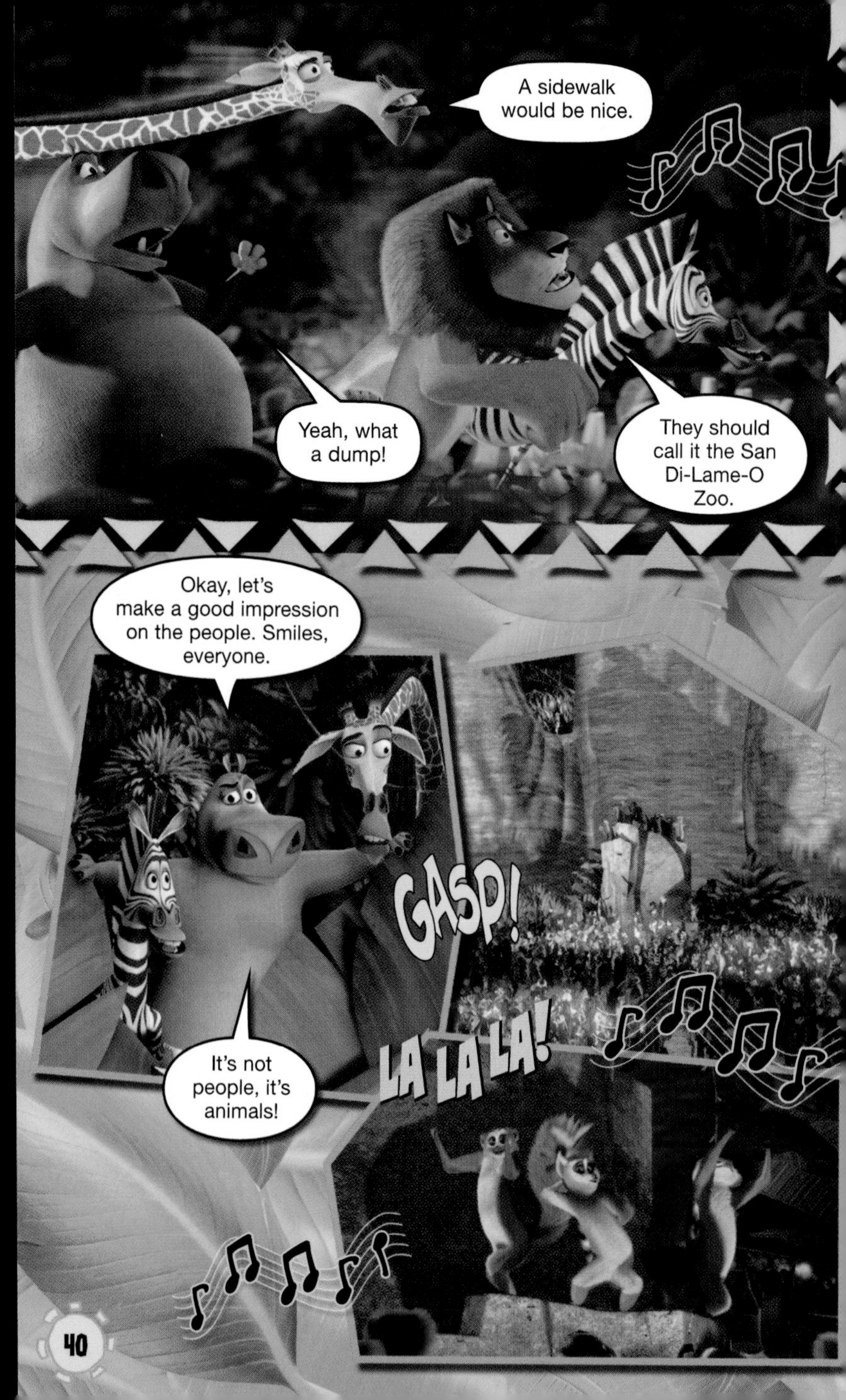
A sidewalk would be nice.
Yeah, what a dump!
They should call it the San Di-Lame-O Zoo.
Okay, let's make a good impression on the people. Smiles, everyone.
GASP!
It's not people, it's animals!
LA LA LA!

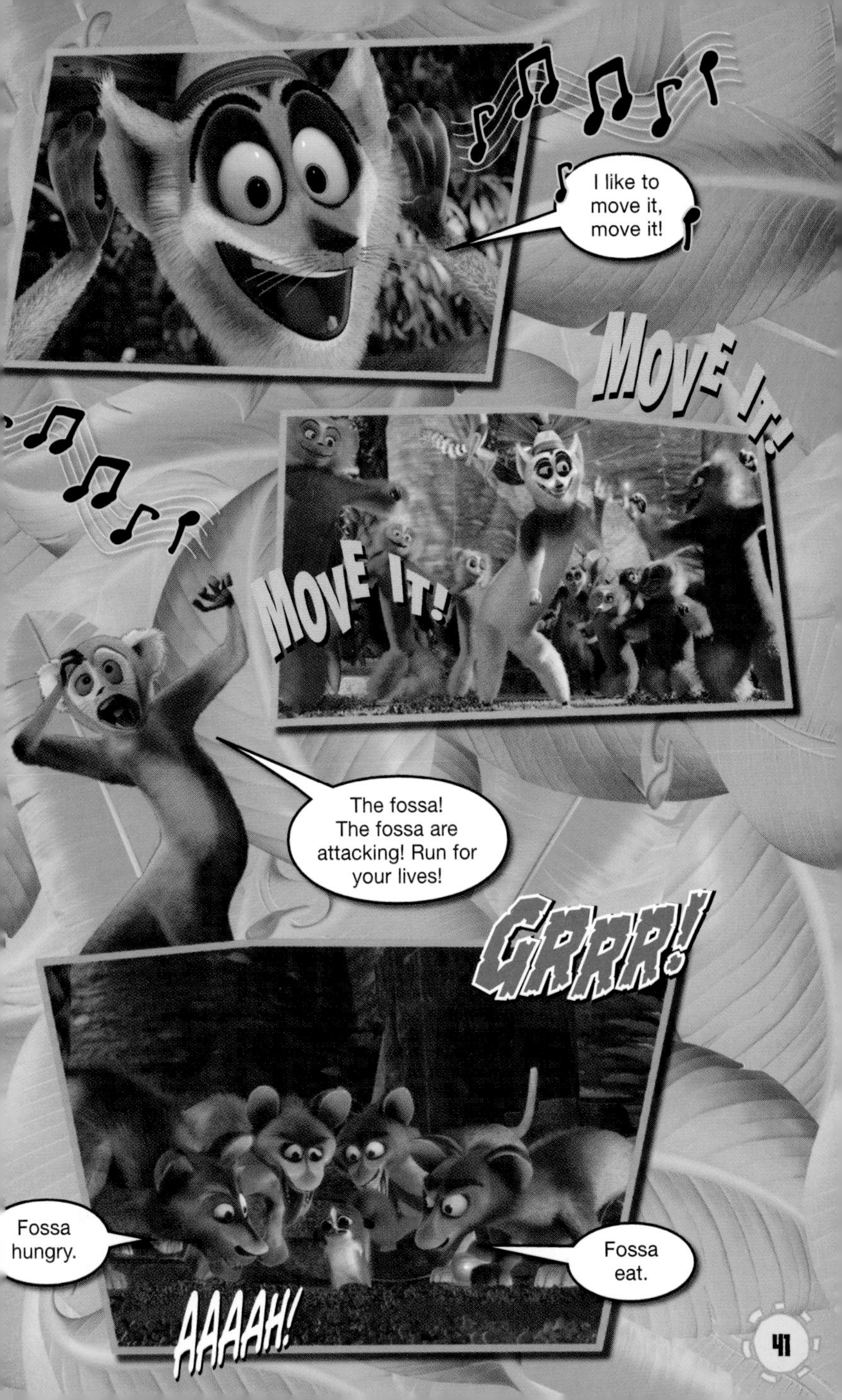
I like to move it, move it!
MOVE IT!
MOVE IT!
The fossa! The fossa are attacking! Run for your lives!
GRRR!
Fossa hungry.
Fossa eat.
AAAAH!

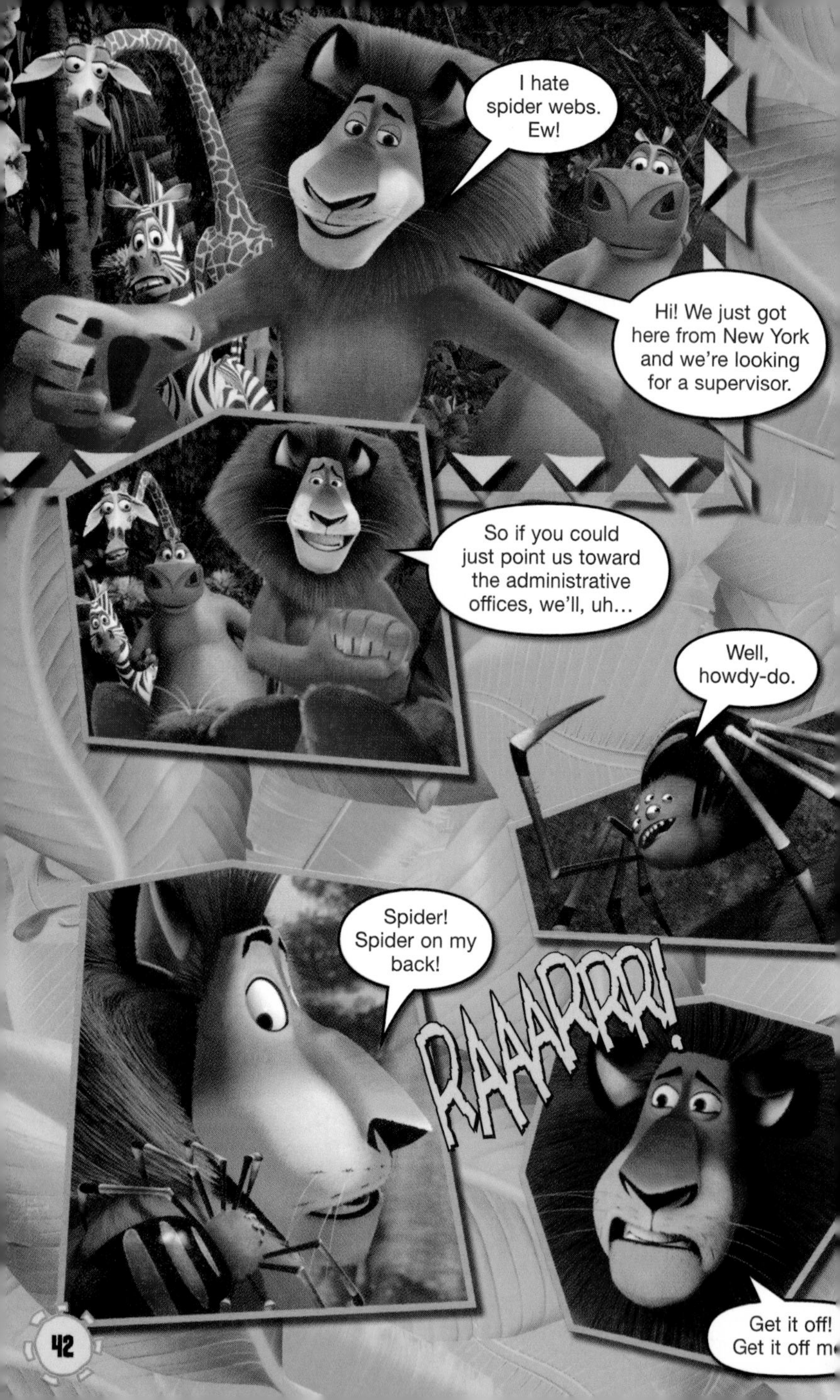
I hate spider webs. Ew!
Hi! We just got here from New York and we're looking for a supervisor.
So if you could just point us toward the administrative offices, we'll, uh…
Well, howdy-do.
Spider! Spider on my back!
RAAARRR!
Get it off! Get it off m

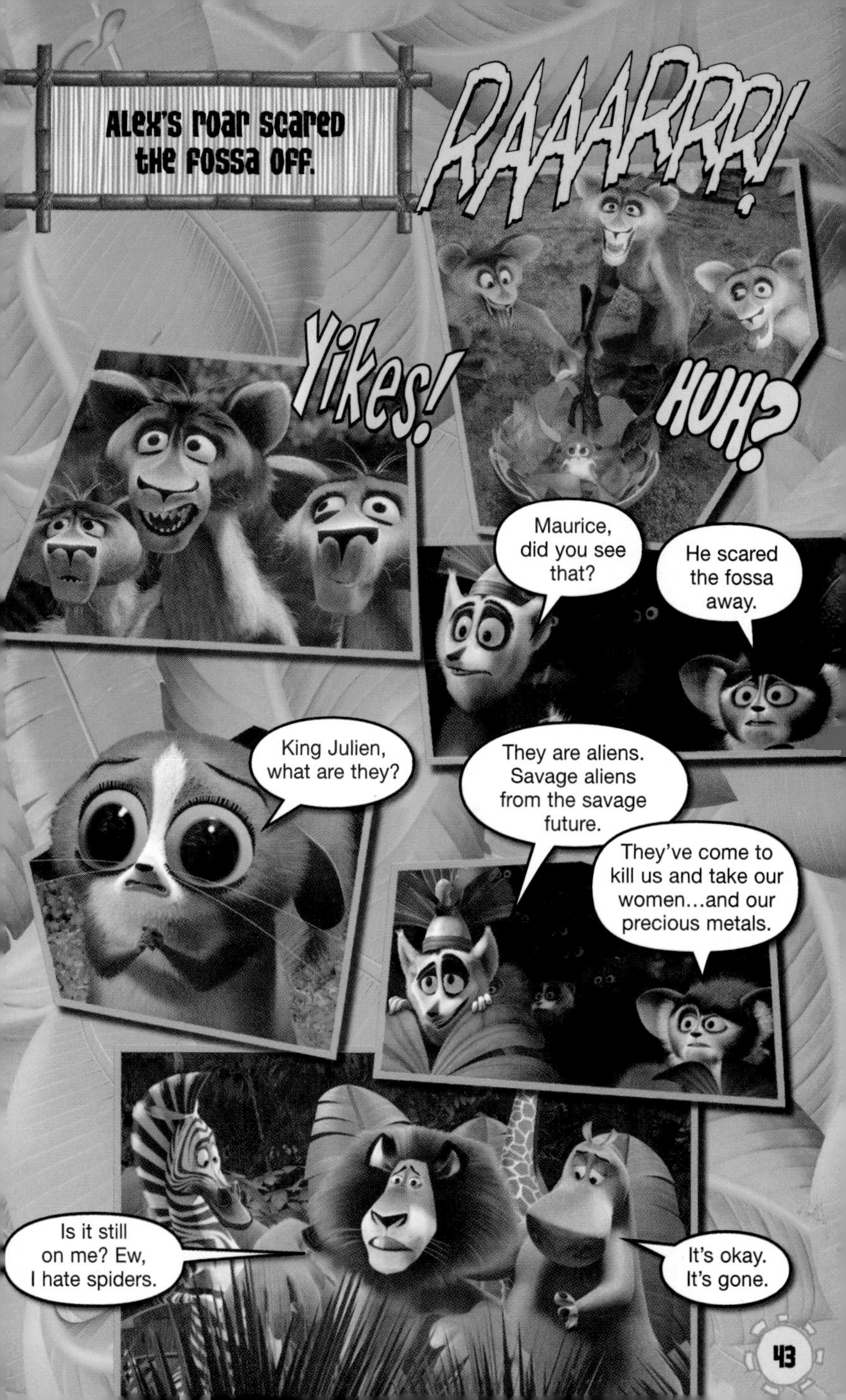

Alex's roar scared the fossa off.
RAAARRR!
Yikes!
HUH?
Maurice, did you see that?
He scared the fossa away.
King Julien, what are they?
They are aliens. Savage aliens from the savage future.
They've come to kill us and take our women…and our precious metals.
Is it still on me? Ew, I hate spiders.
It's okay. It's gone.

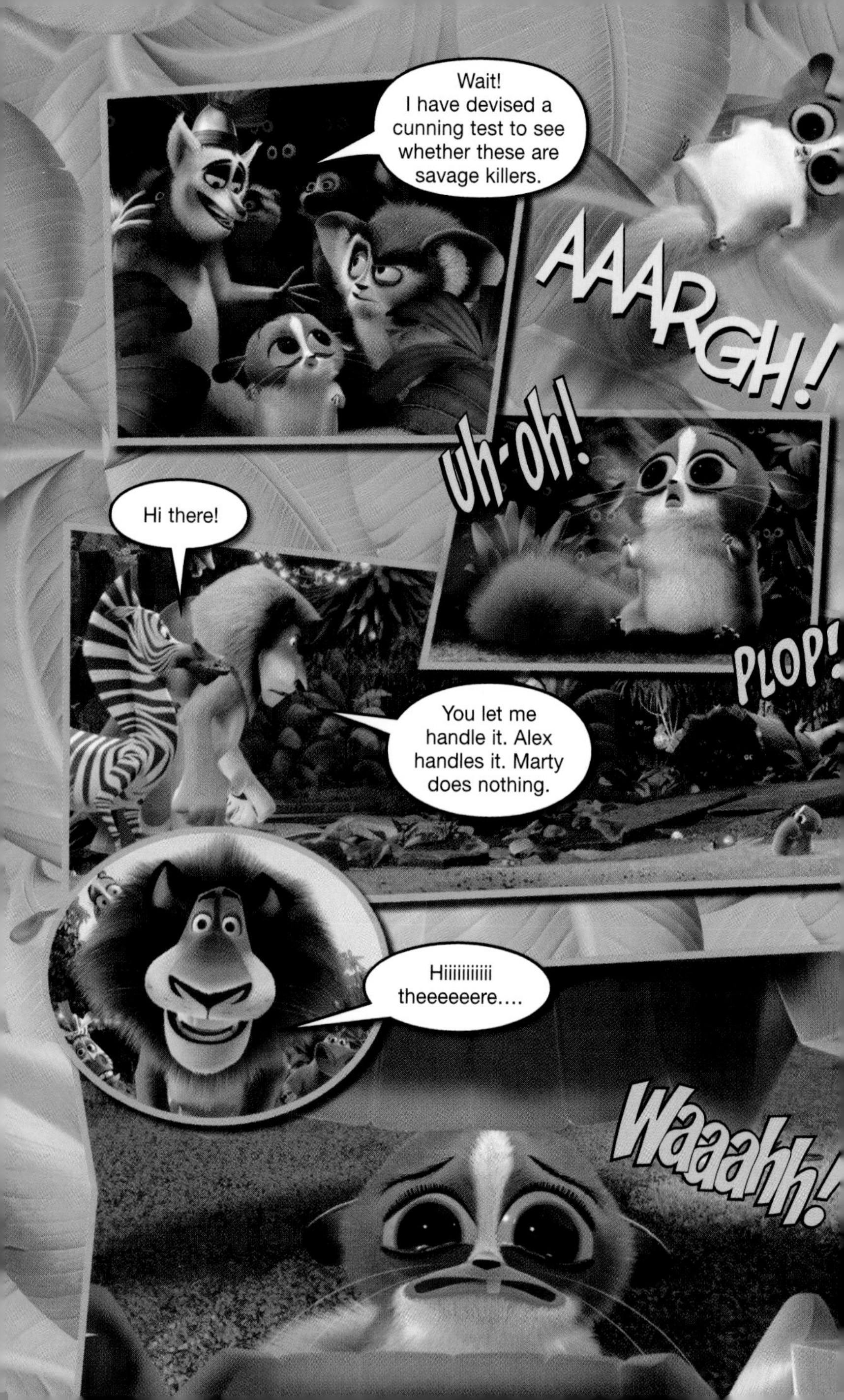
Wait! I have devised a cunning test to see whether these are savage killers.
AAARGH!
Uh-oh!
Hi there!
PLOP!
You let me handle it. Alex handles it. Marty does nothing.
Hiiiiiiiiii theeeeeere....
Waaahh!

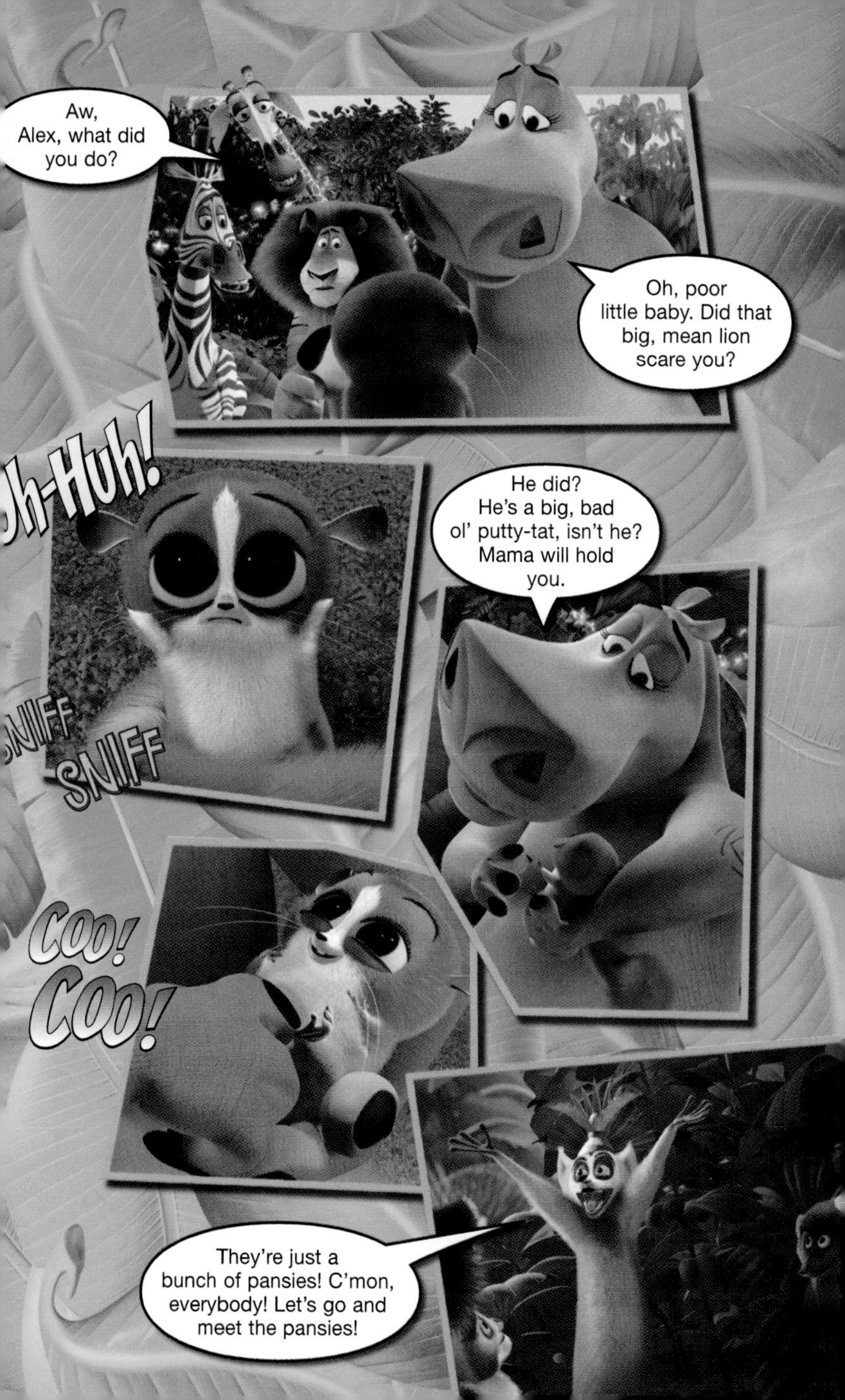
Aw, Alex, what did you do?
Oh, poor little baby. Did that big, mean lion scare you?
Uh-Huh!
SNIFF SNIFF
He did? He's a big, bad ol' putty-tat, isn't he? Mama will hold you.
COO! COO!
They're just a bunch of pansies! C'mon, everybody! Let's go and meet the pansies!

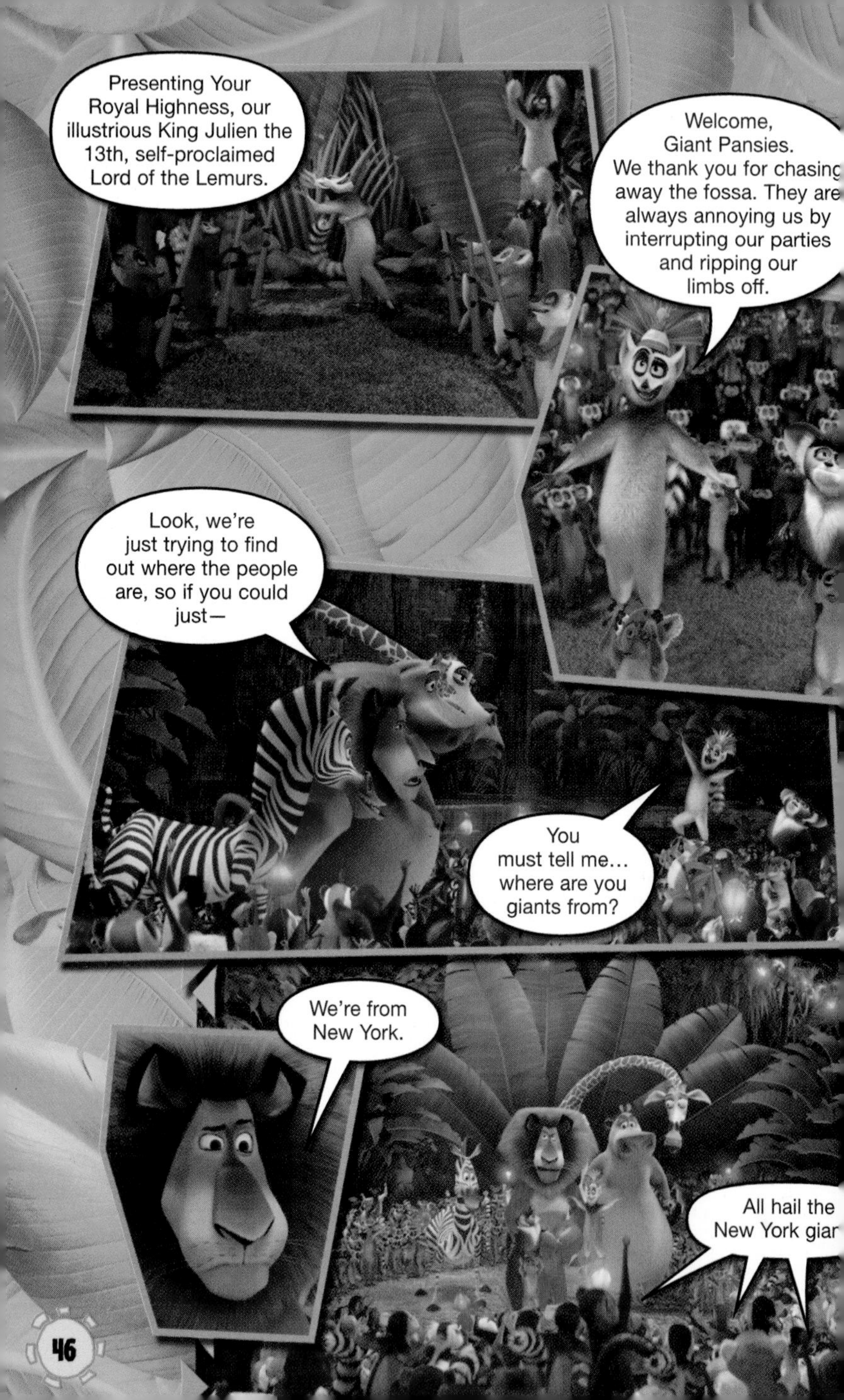
Presenting Your Royal Highness, our illustrious King Julien the 13th, self-proclaimed Lord of the Lemurs.
Welcome, Giant Pansies. We thank you for chasing away the fossa. They are always annoying us by interrupting our parties and ripping our limbs off.
Look, we're just trying to find out where the people are, so if you could just—
You must tell me... where are you giants from?
We're from New York.
All hail the New York gia

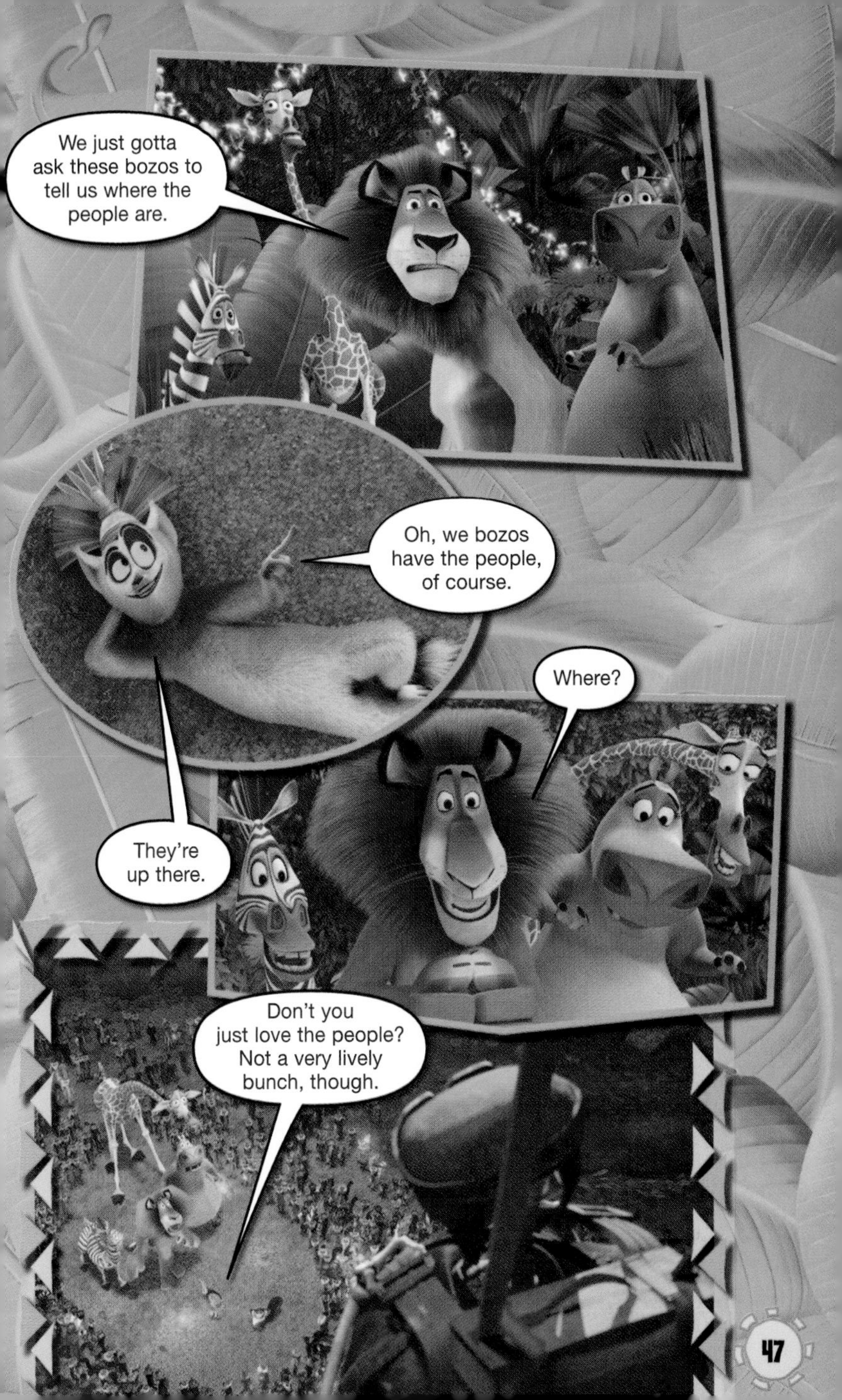
We just gotta ask these bozos to tell us where the people are.
Oh, we bozos have the people, of course.
Where?
They're up there.
Don't you just love the people? Not a very lively bunch, though.

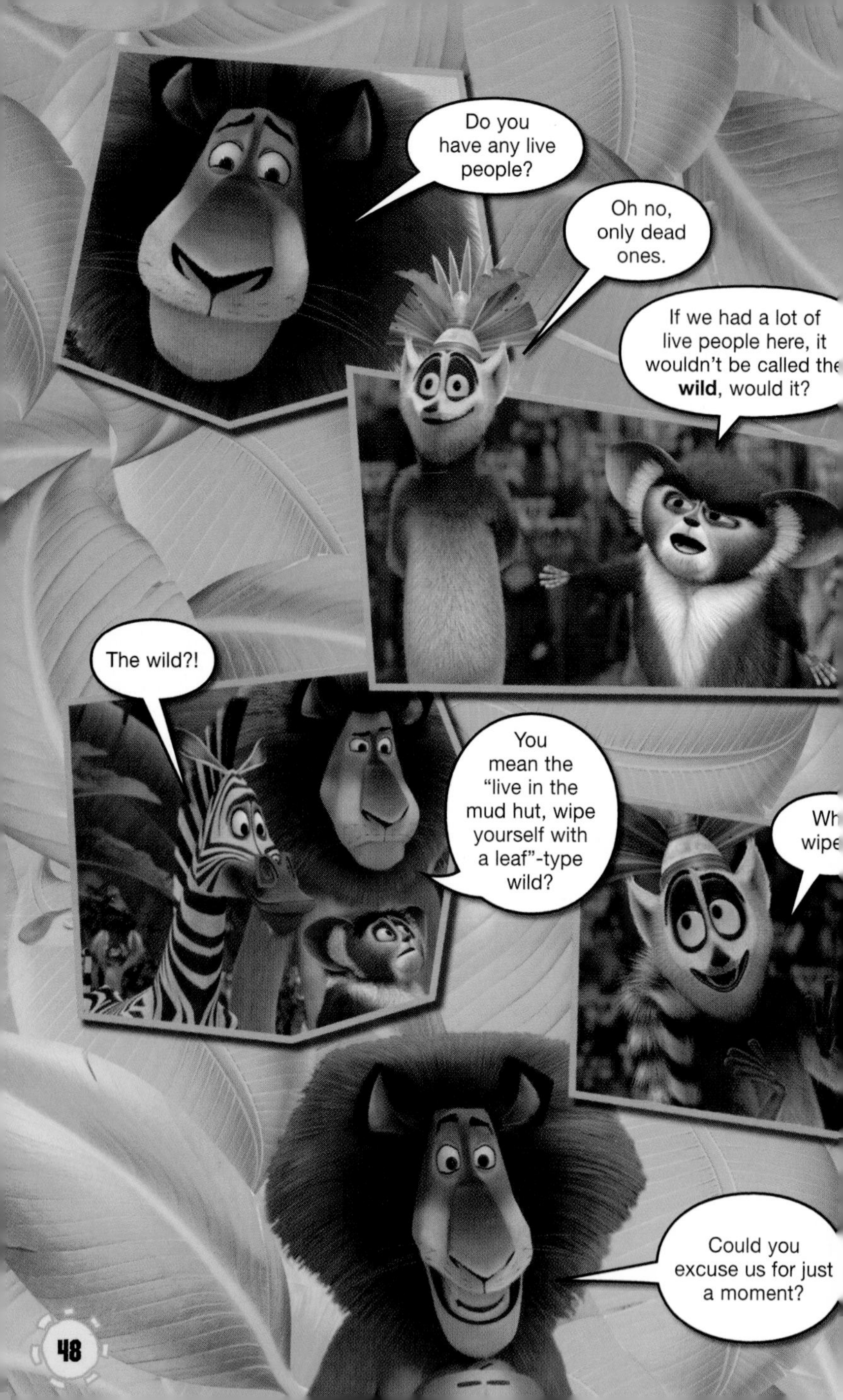
Do you have any live people?
Oh no, only dead ones.
If we had a lot of live people here, it wouldn't be called th **wild**, would it?
The wild?!
You mean the "live in the mud hut, wipe yourself with a leaf"-type wild?
Could you excuse us for just a moment?

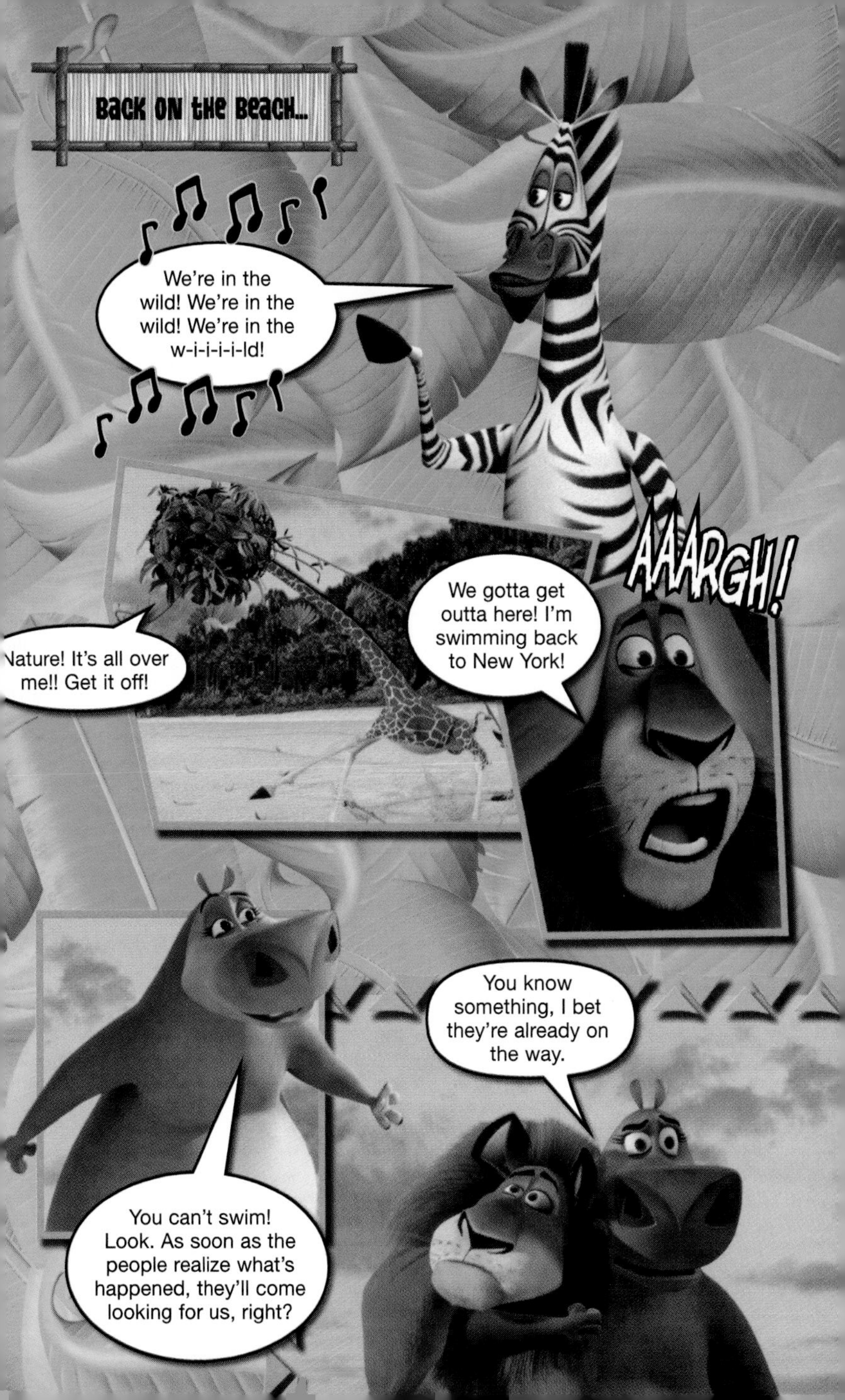
Back on the Beach...
We're in the wild! We're in the wild! We're in the w-i-i-i-i-ld!
Nature! It's all over me!! Get it off!
AAARGH!
We gotta get outta here! I'm swimming back to New York!
You can't swim! Look. As soon as the people realize what's happened, they'll come looking for us, right?
You know something, I bet they're already on the way.

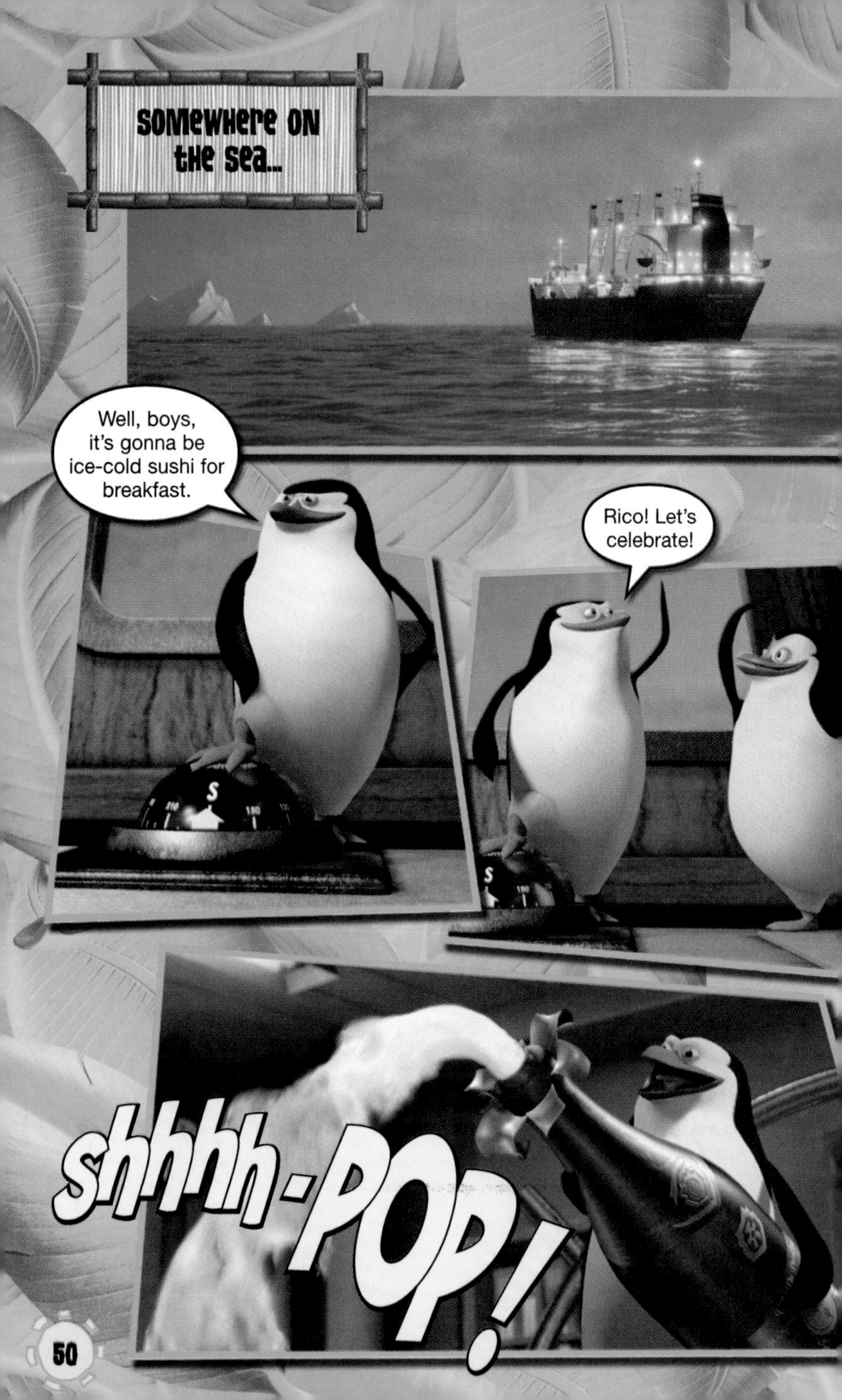

SOMEWHERE ON THE SEA...
Well, boys, it's gonna be ice-cold sushi for breakfast.
Rico! Let's celebrate!
shhhh-POP!

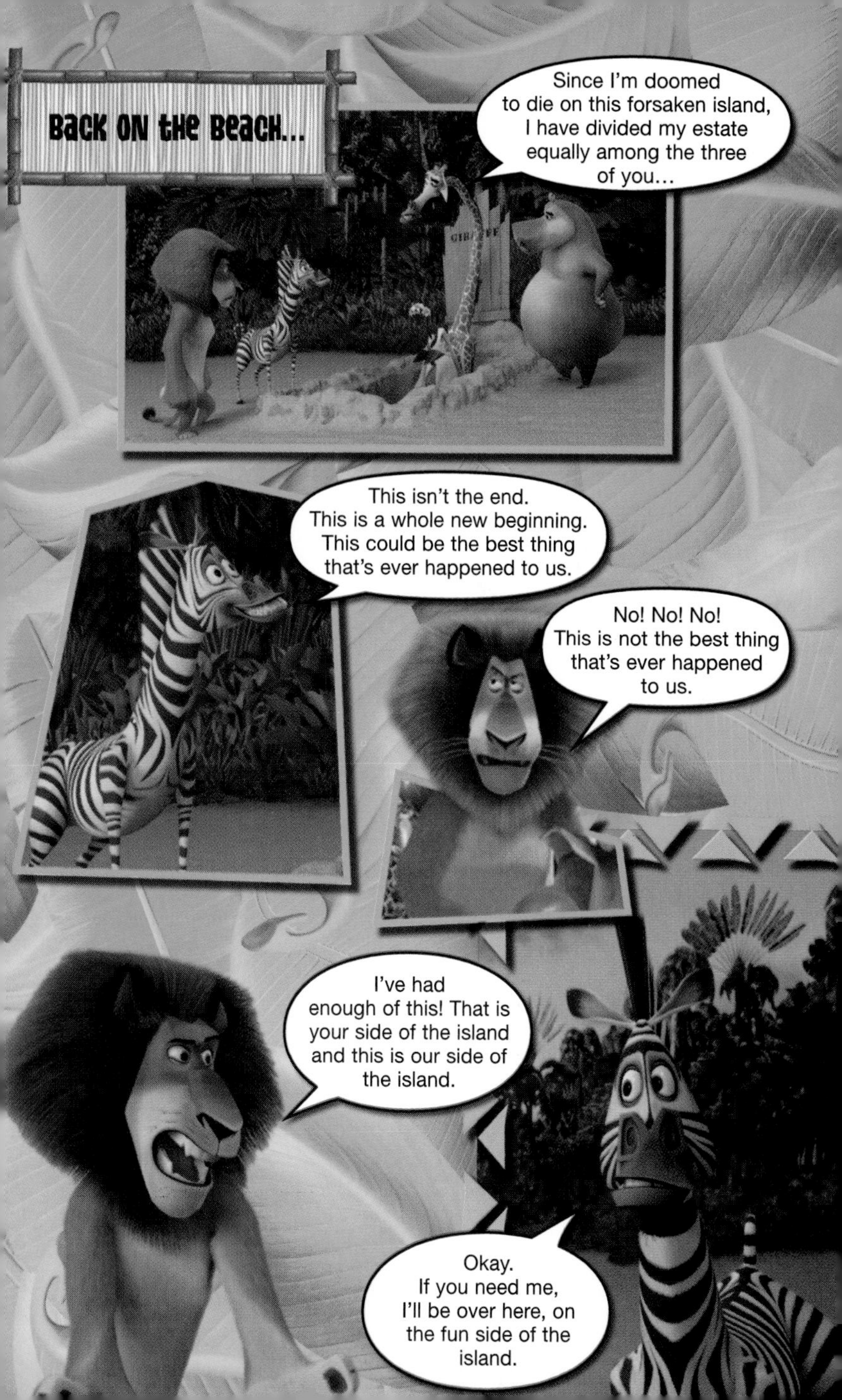
BACK ON THE BEACH...
Since I'm doomed to die on this forsaken island, I have divided my estate equally among the three of you...
This isn't the end. This is a whole new beginning. This could be the best thing that's ever happened to us.
No! No! No! This is not the best thing that's ever happened to us.
I've had enough of this! That is your side of the island and this is our side of the island.
Okay. If you need me, I'll be over here, on the fun side of the island.

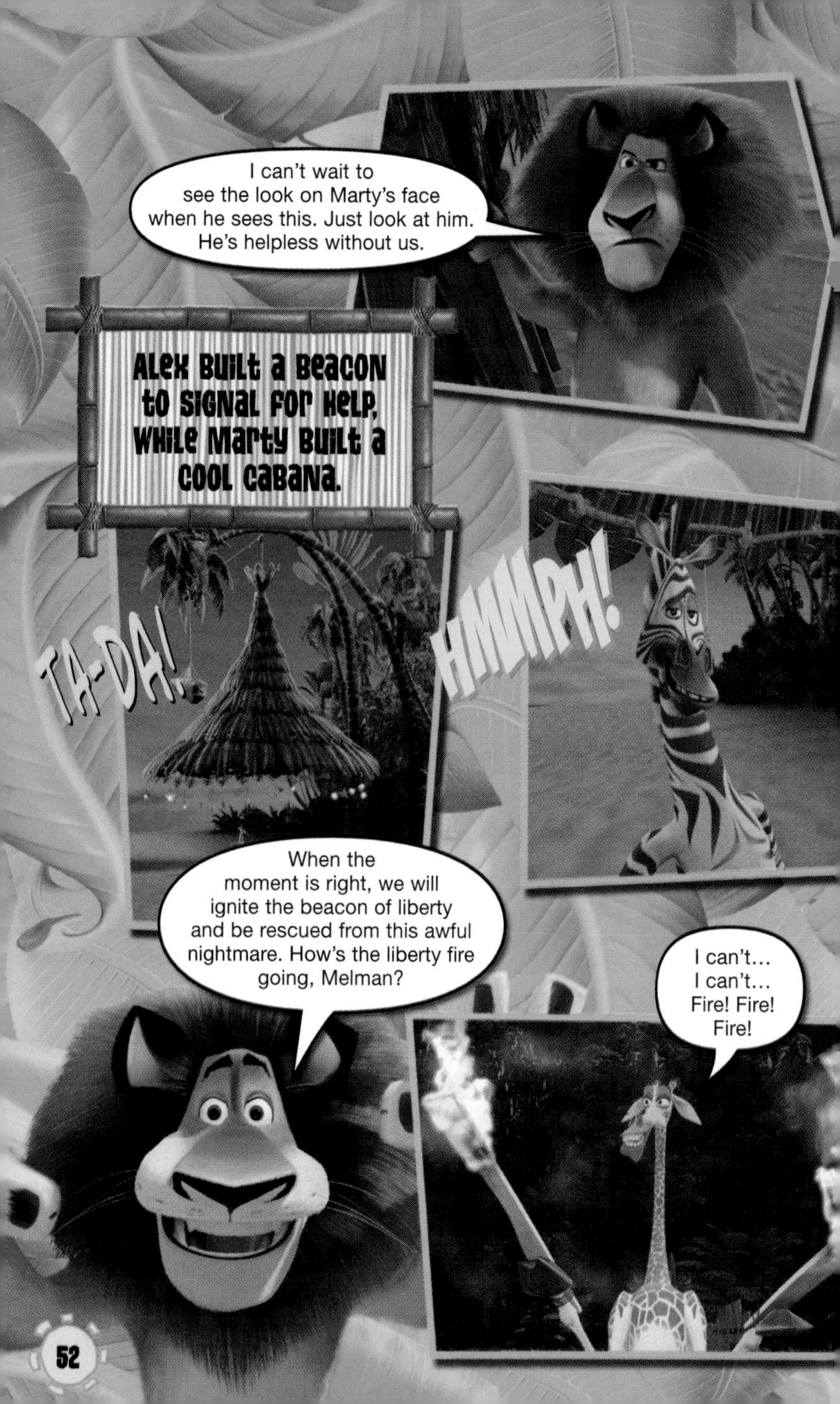
I can't wait to see the look on Marty's face when he sees this. Just look at him. He's helpless without us.
ALEX BUILT A BEACON TO SIGNAL FOR HELP, WHILE MARTY BUILT A COOL CABANA.
TA-DA!
HMMPH!
When the moment is right, we will ignite the beacon of liberty and be rescued from this awful nightmare. How's the liberty fire going, Melman?
I can't... I can't... Fire! Fire! Fire!

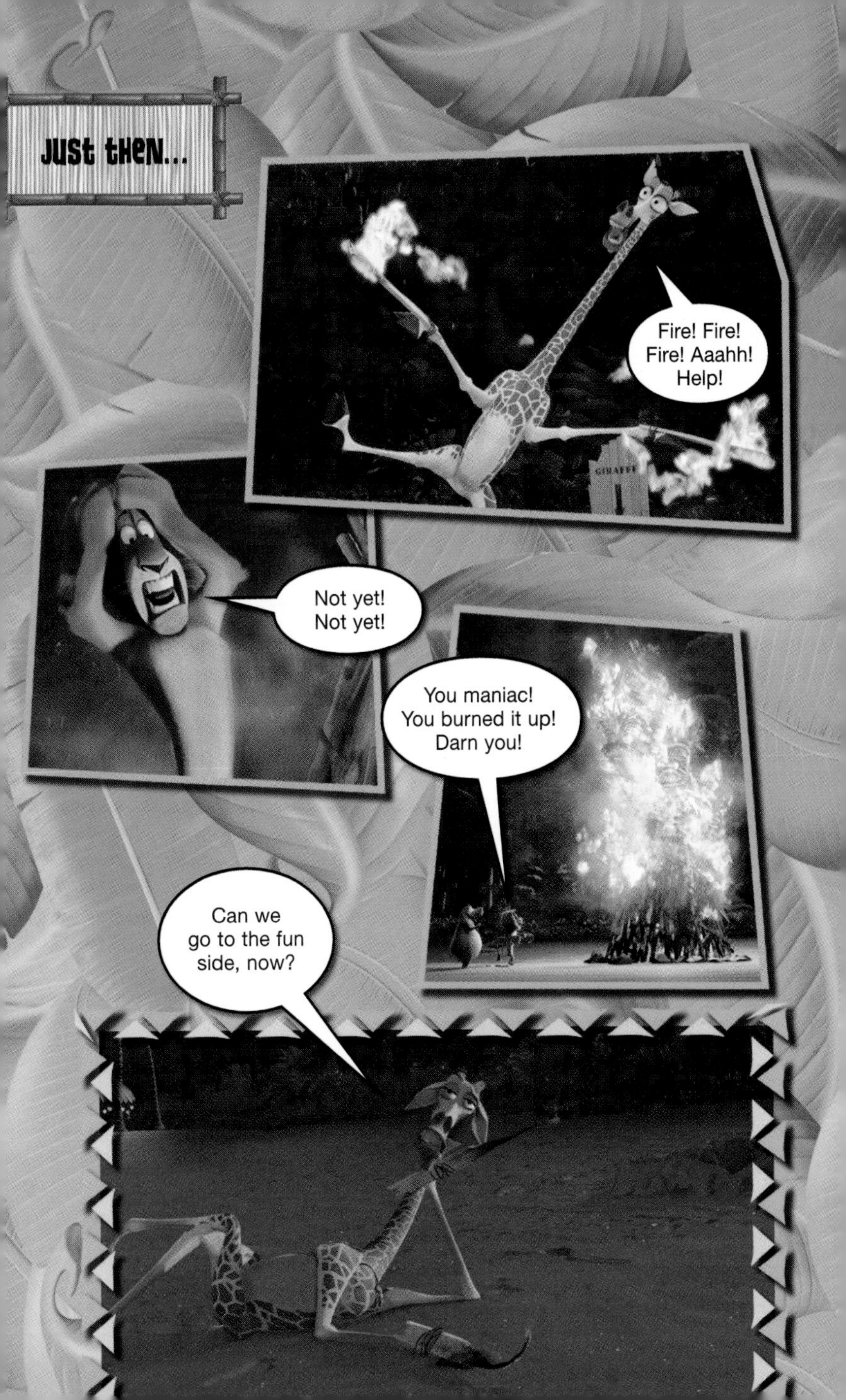
Just then...
Fire! Fire! Fire! Aaahh! Help!
Not yet! Not yet!
You maniac! You burned it up! Darn you!
Can we go to the fun side, now?

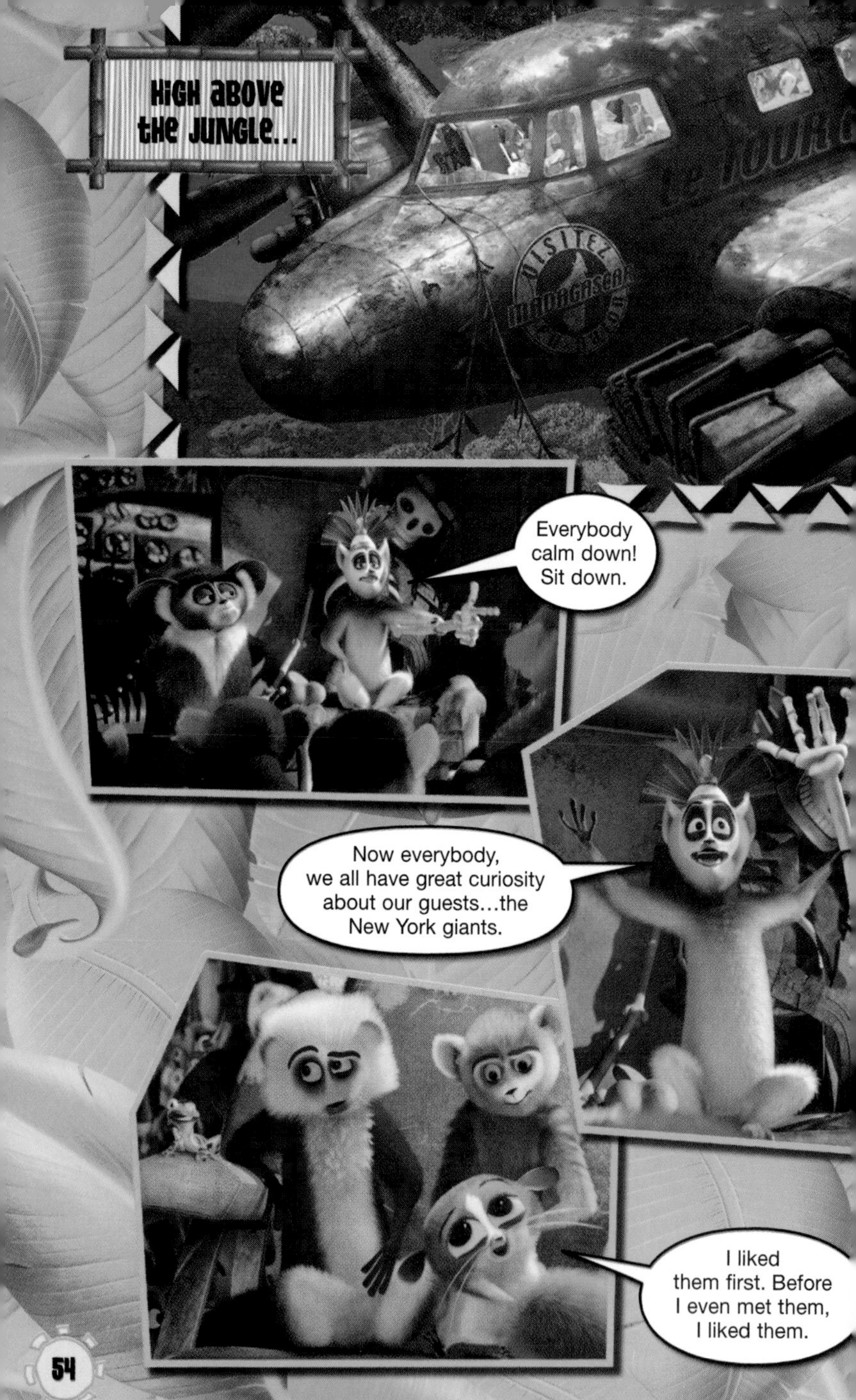

HIGH ABOVE THE JUNGLE...
Everybody calm down! Sit down.
Now everybody, we all have great curiosity about our guests...the New York giants.
I liked them first. Before I even met them, I liked them.

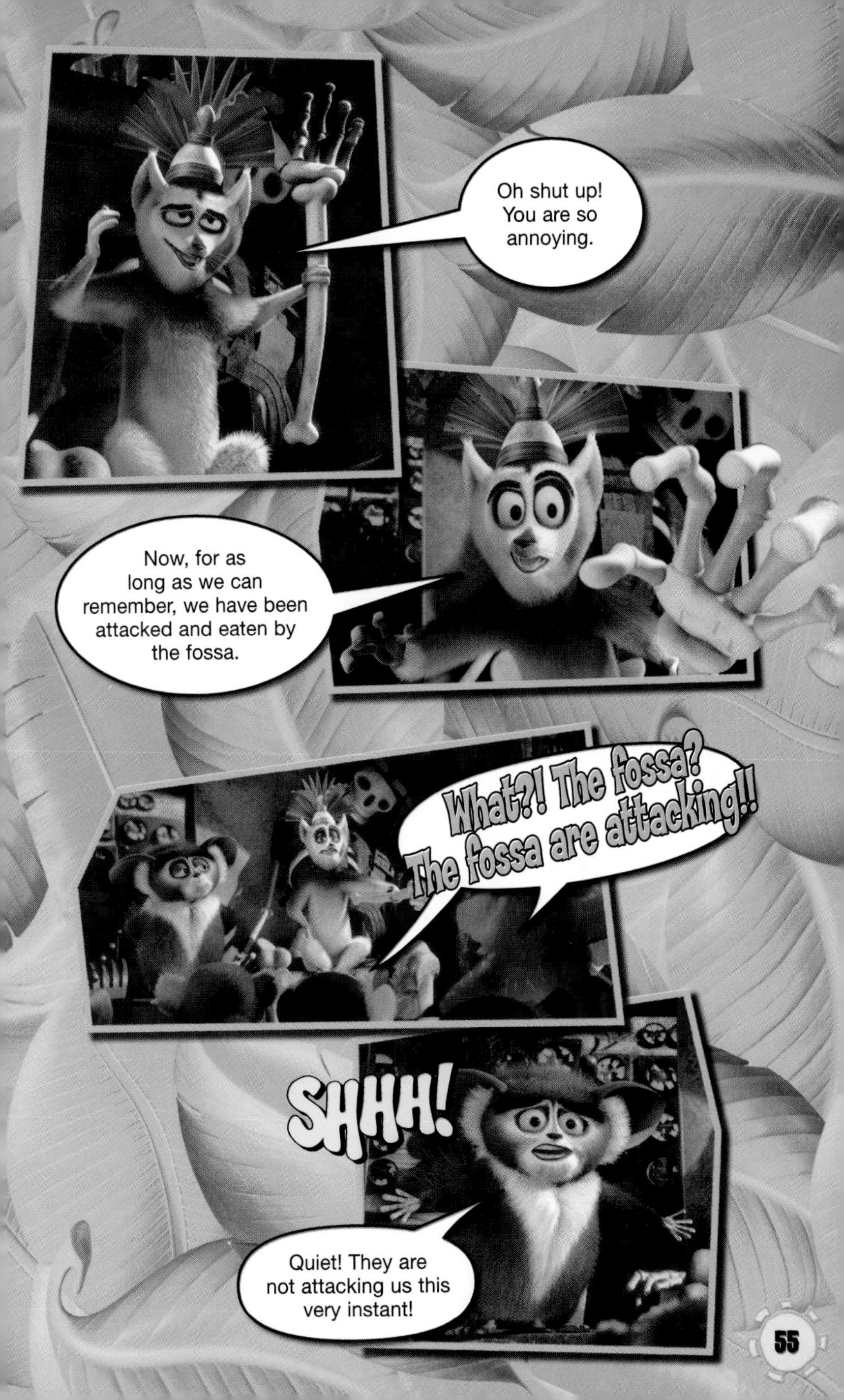
Oh shut up! You are so annoying.
Now, for as long as we can remember, we have been attacked and eaten by the fossa.
What?! The fossa? The fossa are attacking!!
SHHH!
Quiet! They are not attacking us this very instant!

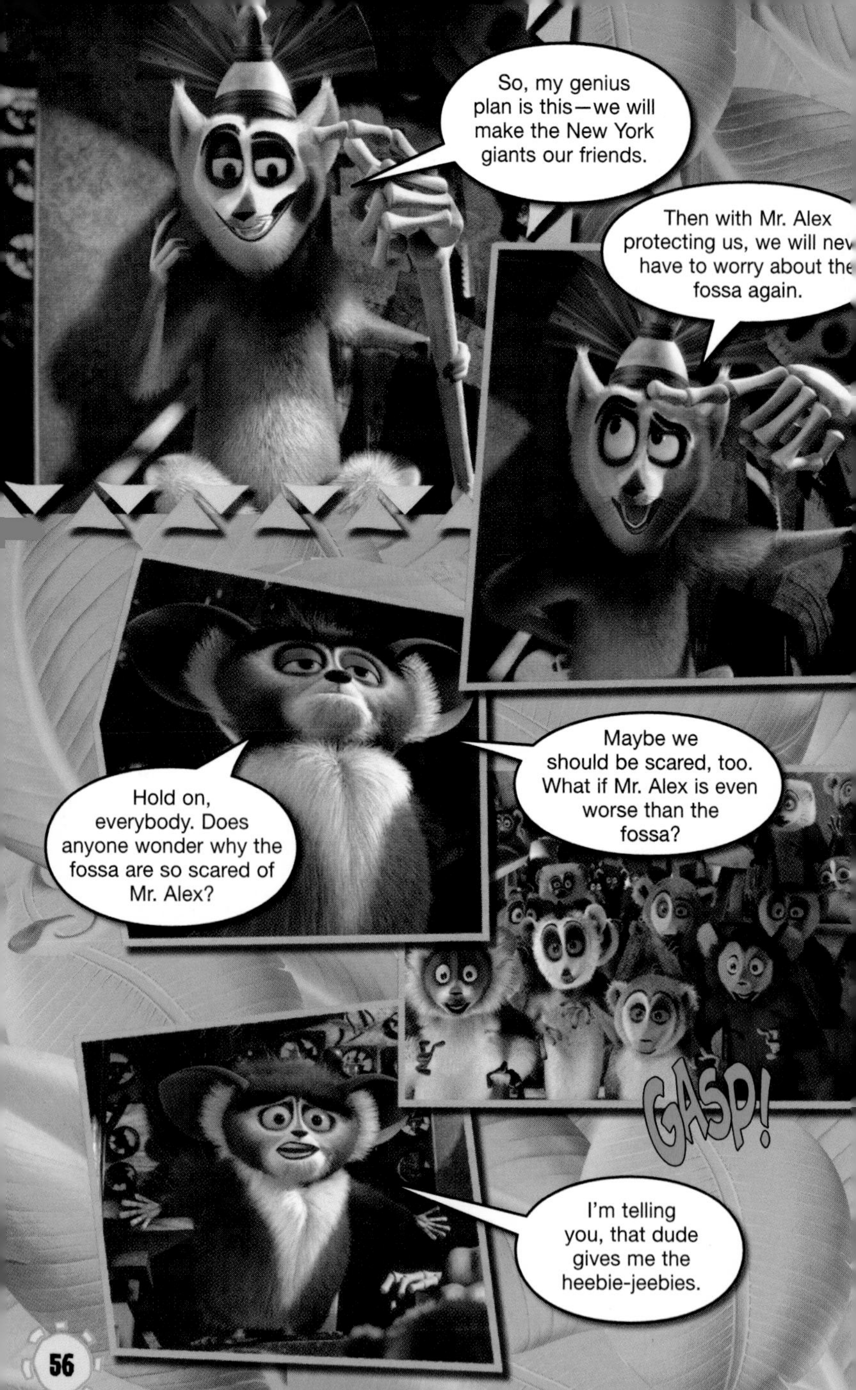
So, my genius plan is this—we will make the New York giants our friends.
Then with Mr. Alex protecting us, we will nev have to worry about the fossa again.
Hold on, everybody. Does anyone wonder why the fossa are so scared of Mr. Alex?
Maybe we should be scared, too. What if Mr. Alex is even worse than the fossa?
GASP!
I'm telling you, that dude gives me the heebie-jeebies.

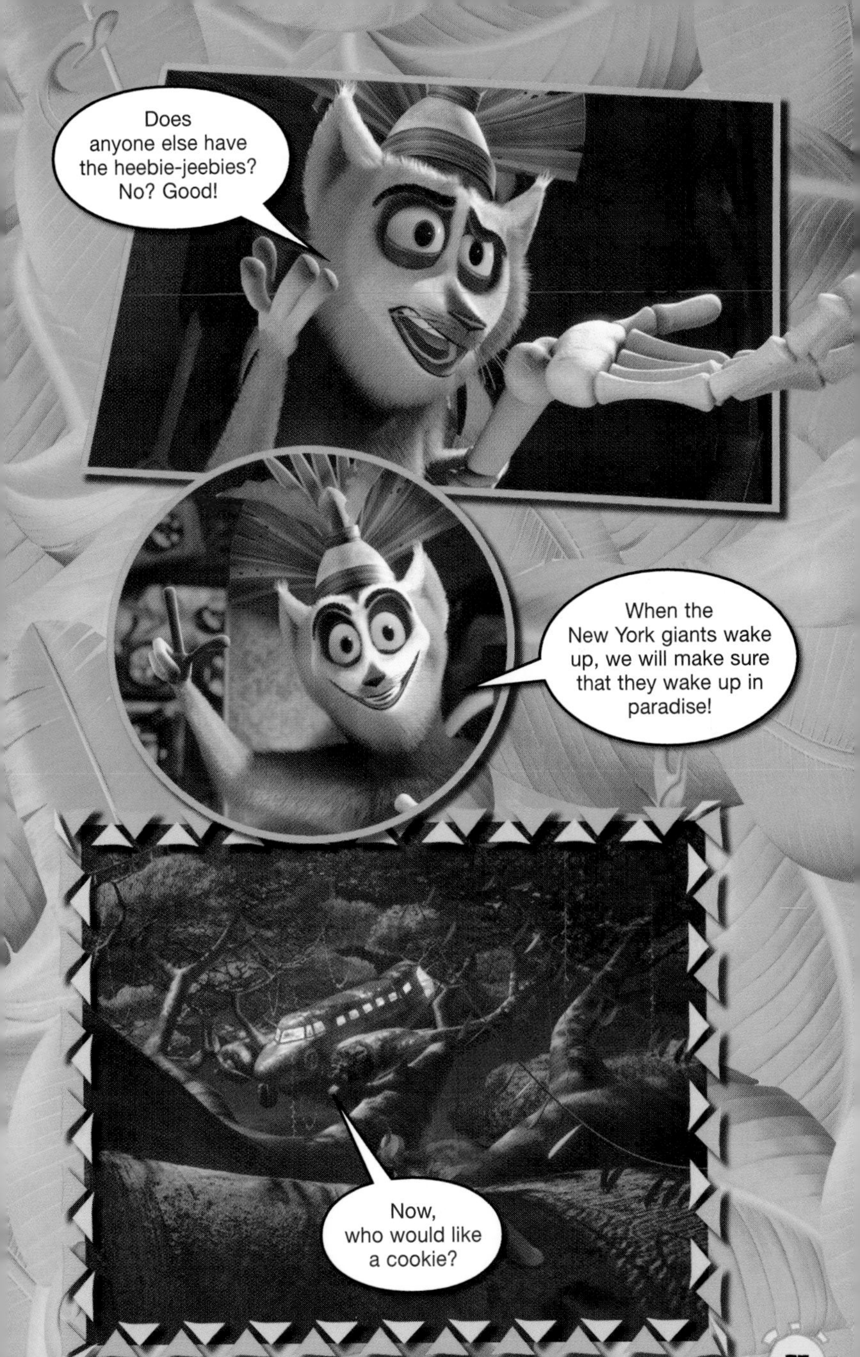
Does anyone else have the heebie-jeebies? No? Good!
When the New York giants wake up, we will make sure that they wake up in paradise!
Now, who would like a cookie?

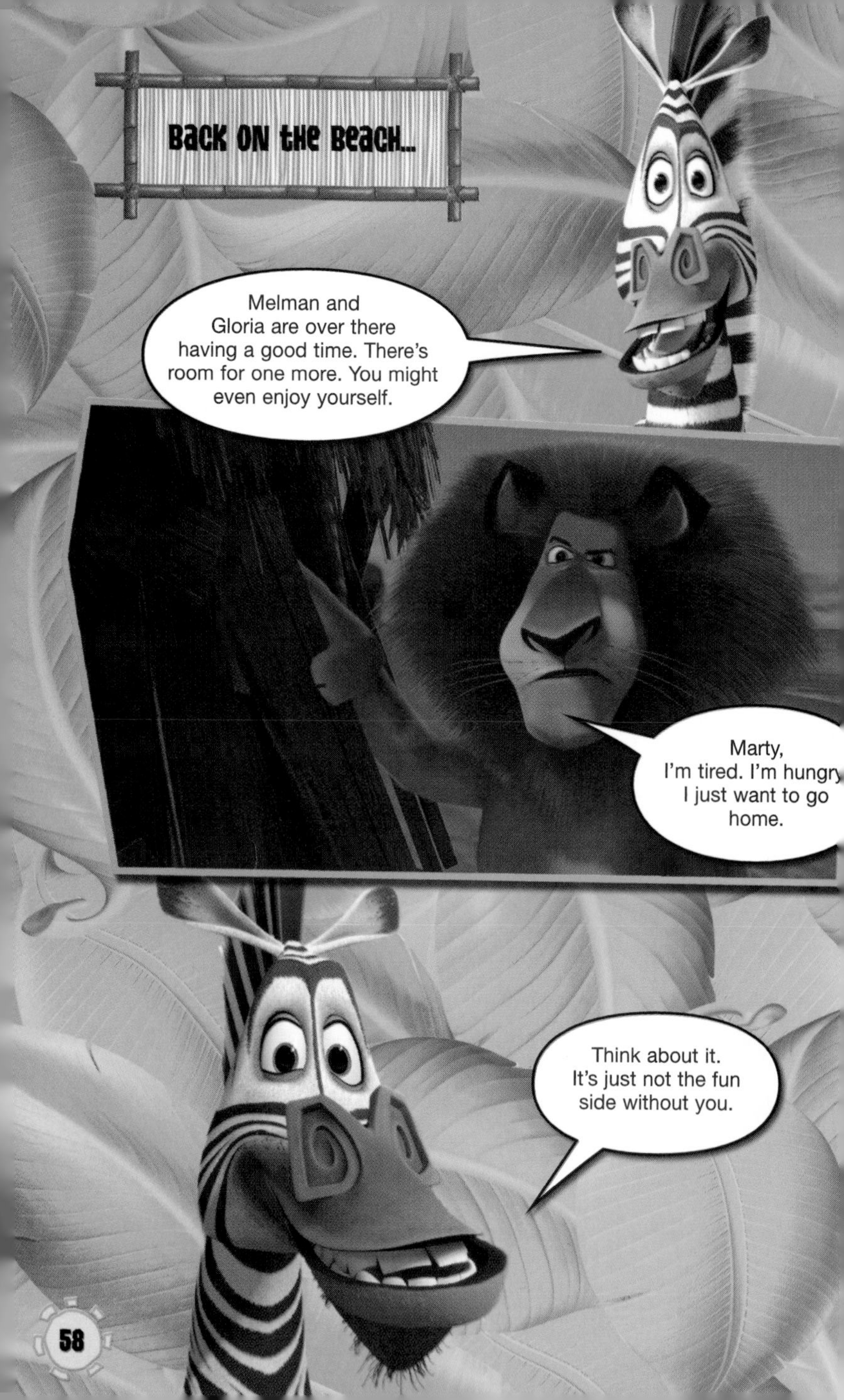
Back on the Beach...
Melman and Gloria are over there having a good time. There's room for one more. You might even enjoy yourself.
Marty, I'm tired. I'm hungry. I just want to go home.
Think about it. It's just not the fun side without you.

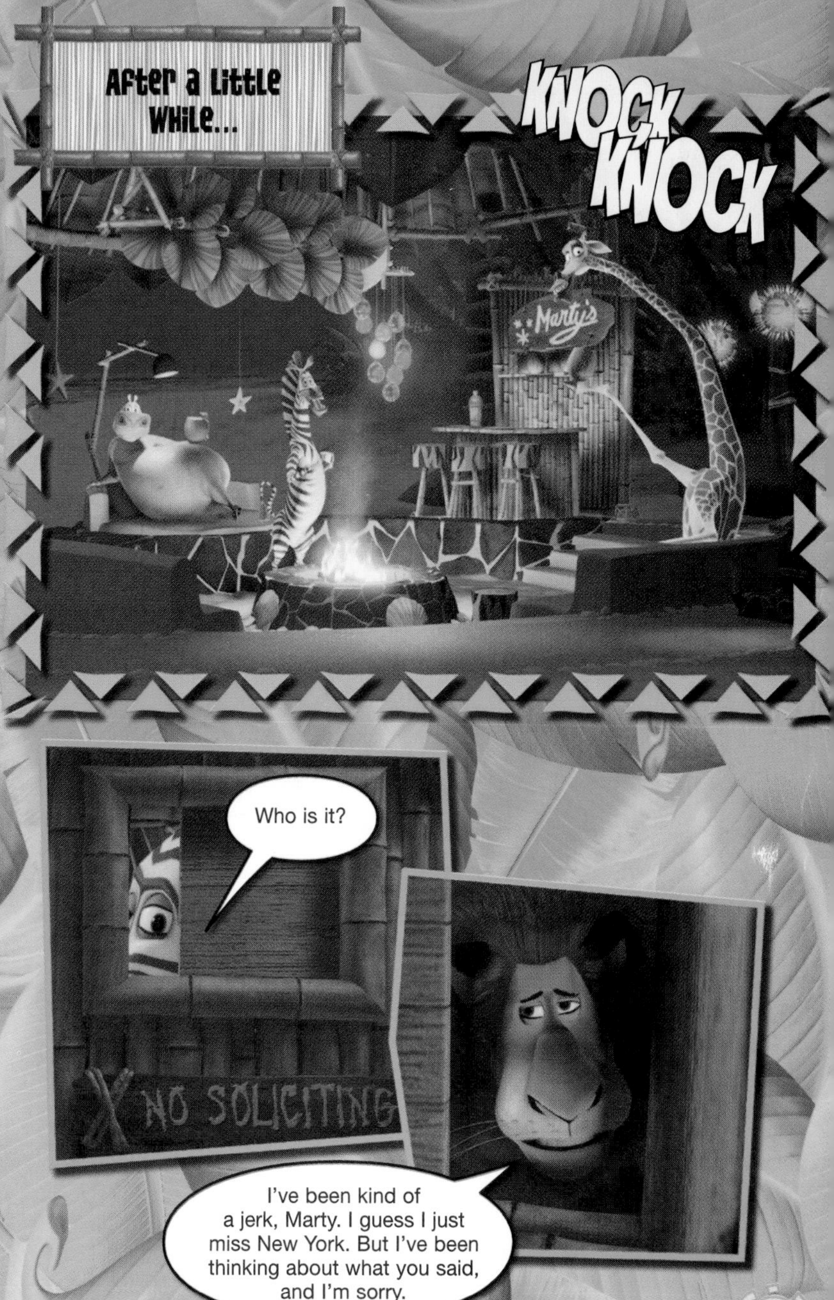
After a Little While...
KNOCK KNOCK
Marty's
Who is it?
NO SOLICITING
I've been kind of a jerk, Marty. I guess I just miss New York. But I've been thinking about what you said, and I'm sorry.

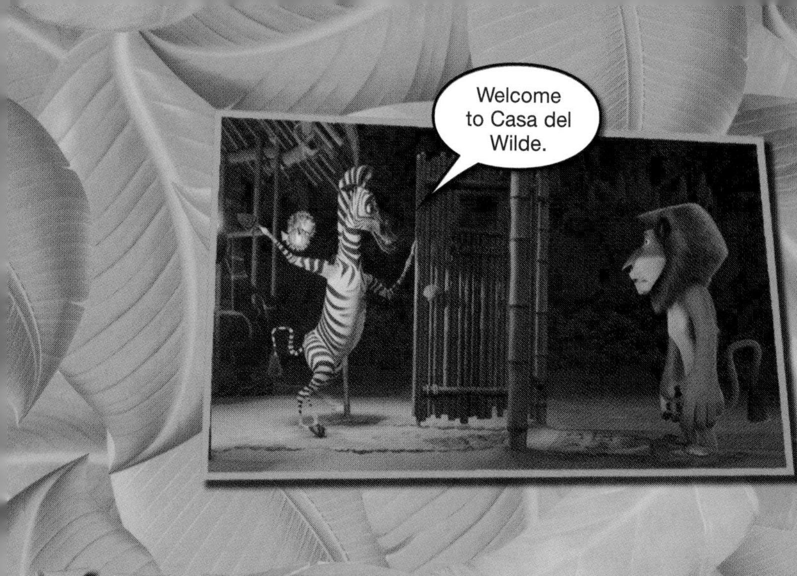
Welcome to Casa del Wilde.

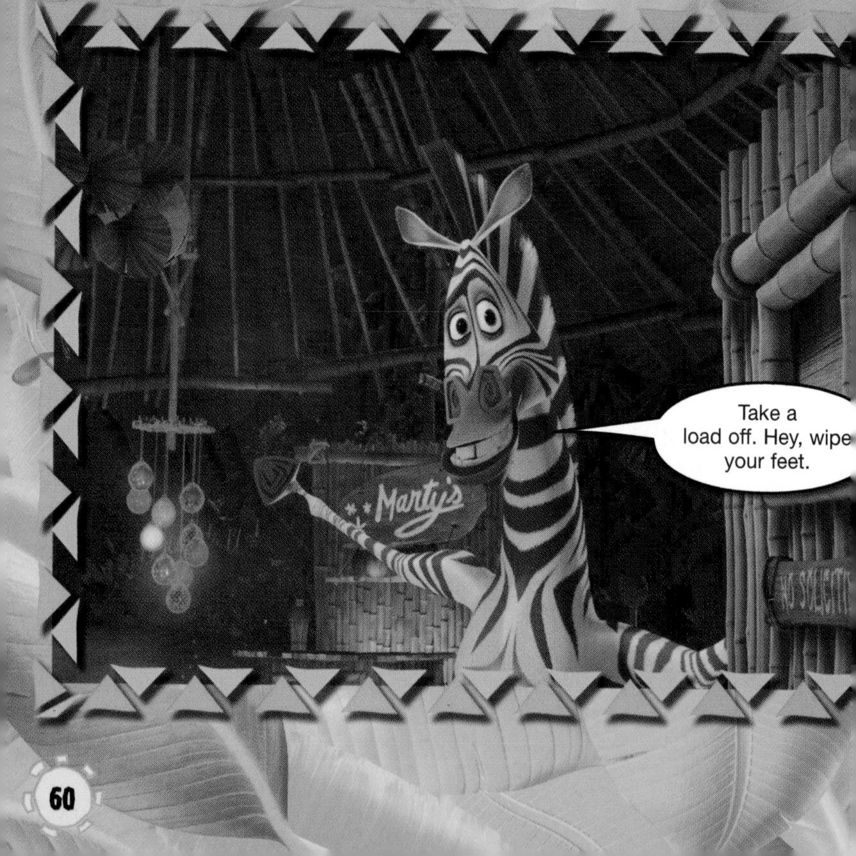
Marty's
Take a load off. Hey, wipe your feet.

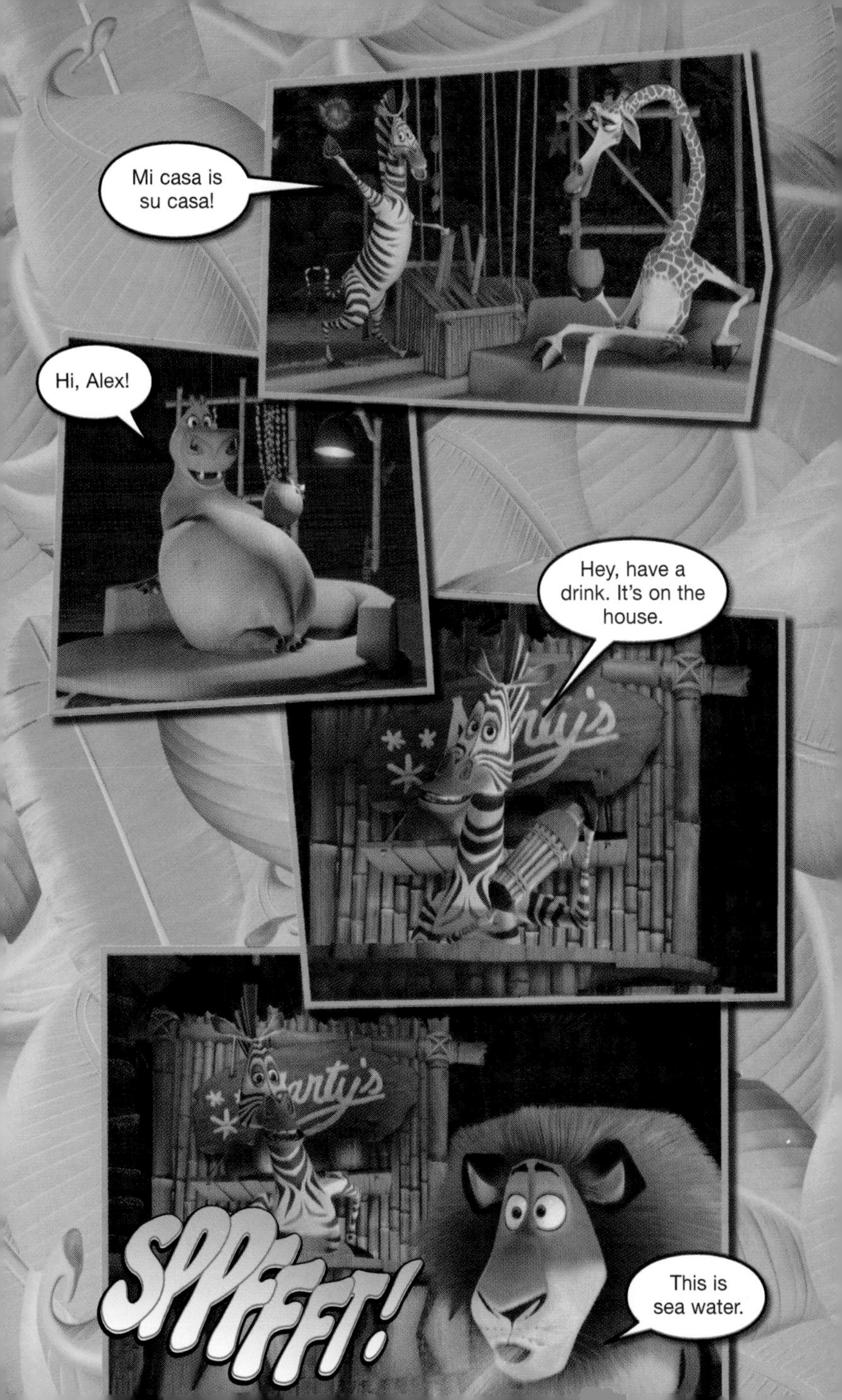
Mi casa is su casa!
Hi, Alex!
Hey, have a drink. It's on the house.
SPPFFFT!
This is sea water.

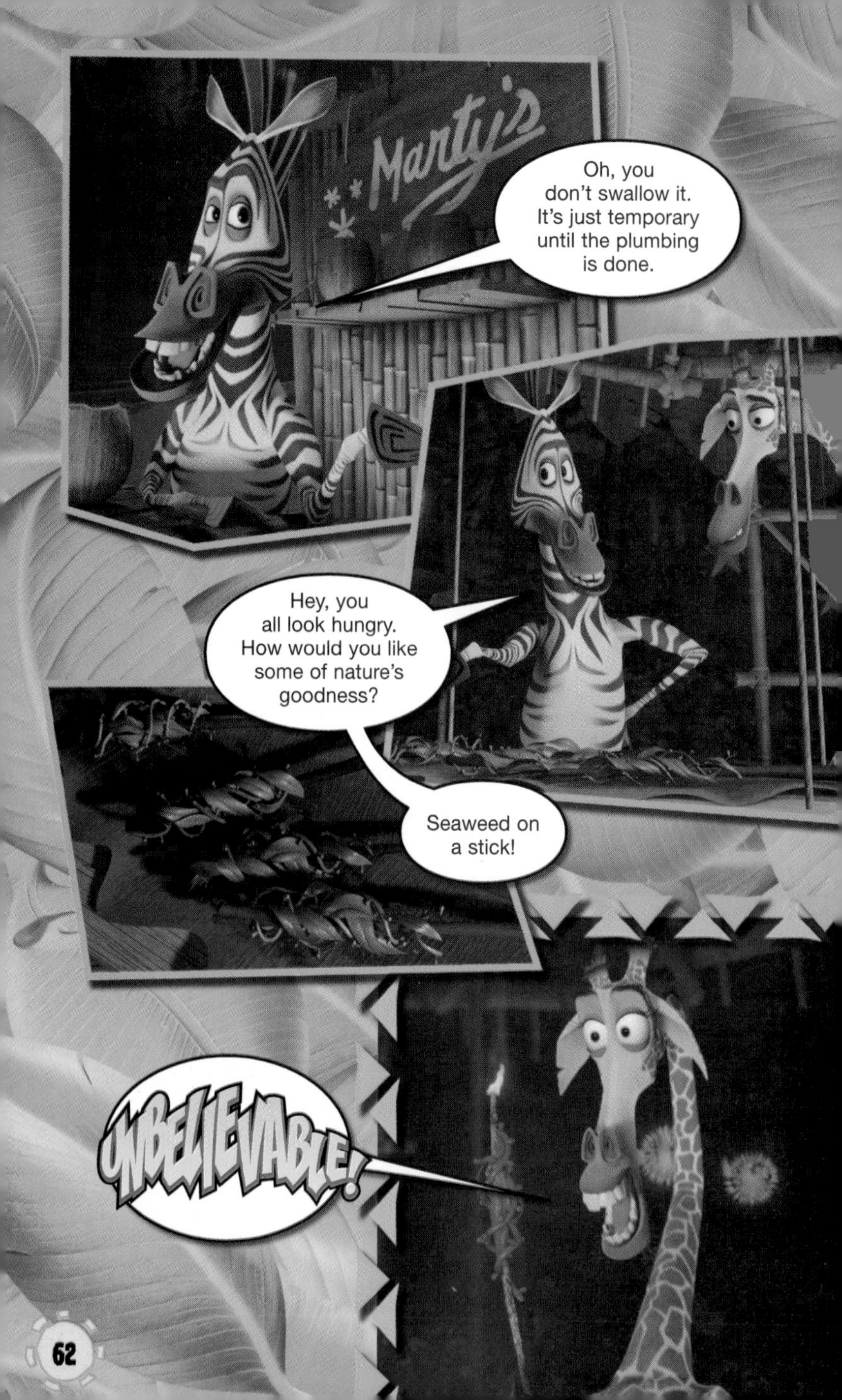
Marty's
Oh, you don't swallow it. It's just temporary until the plumbing is done.
Hey, you all look hungry. How would you like some of nature's goodness?
Seaweed on a stick!
UNBELIEVABLE!

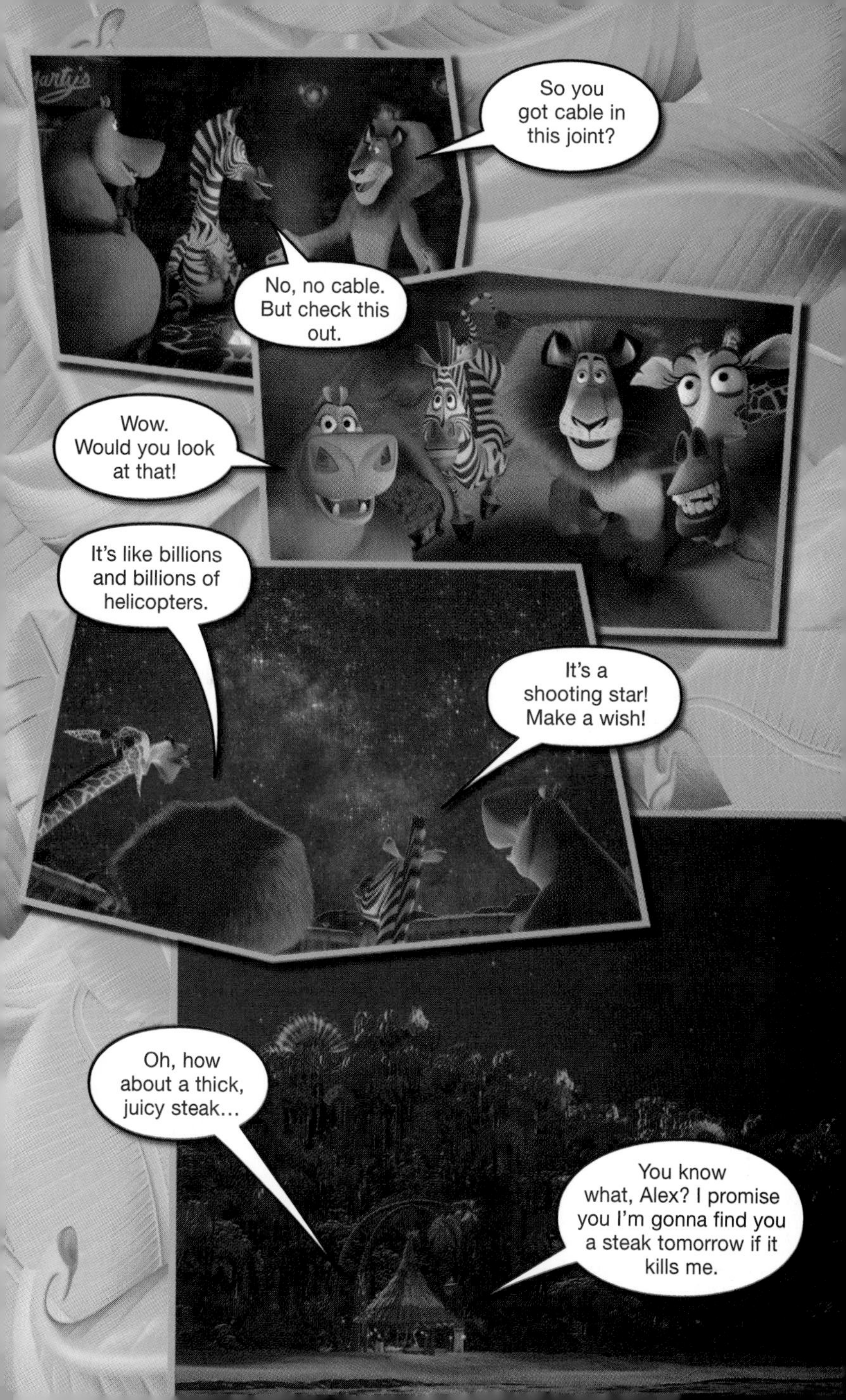
So you got cable in this joint?
No, no cable. But check this out.
Wow. Would you look at that!
It's like billions and billions of helicopters.
It's a shooting star! Make a wish!
Oh, how about a thick, juicy steak…
You know what, Alex? I promise you I'm gonna find you a steak tomorrow if it kills me.

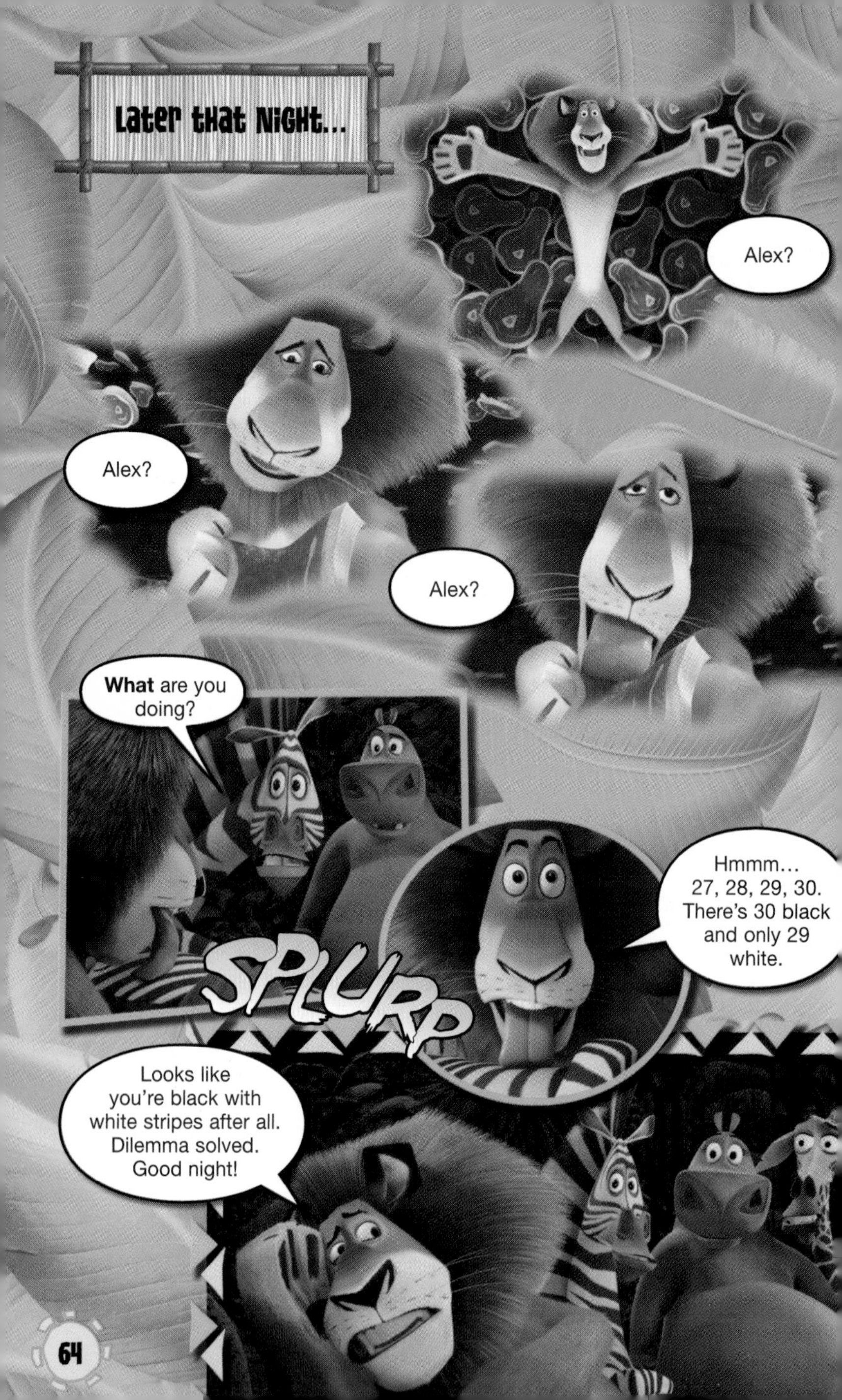

Later that Night...
Alex?
Alex?
Alex?
What are you doing?
Hmmm… 27, 28, 29, 30. There's 30 black and only 29 white.
SPLURP
Looks like you're black with white stripes after all. Dilemma solved. Good night!

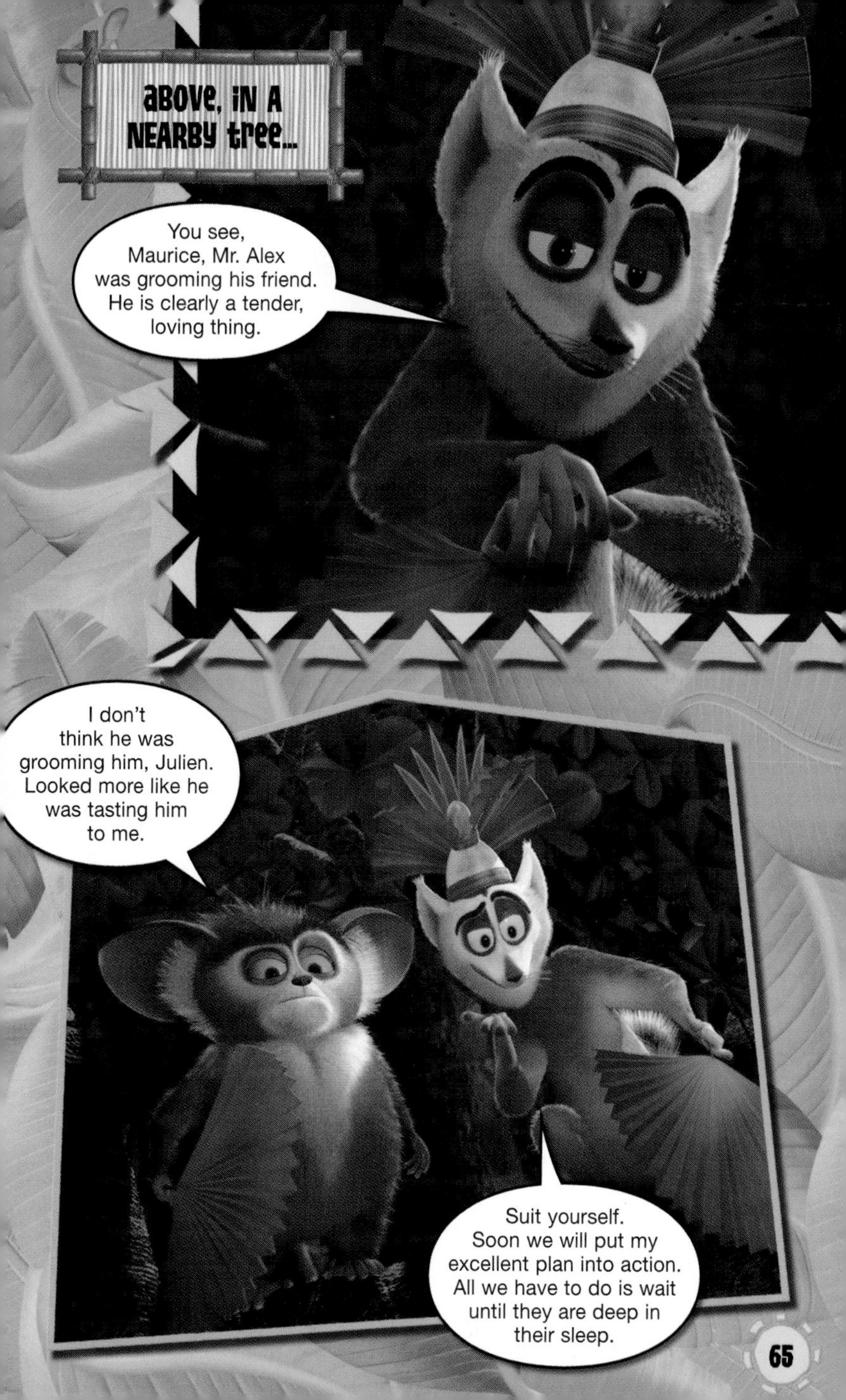
ABOVE, IN A NEARBY TREE...
You see, Maurice, Mr. Alex was grooming his friend. He is clearly a tender, loving thing.
I don't think he was grooming him, Julien. Looked more like he was tasting him to me.
Suit yourself. Soon we will put my excellent plan into action. All we have to do is wait until they are deep in their sleep.

MEANWHILE, iN
ANTARCTICA...

Well, this sucks.

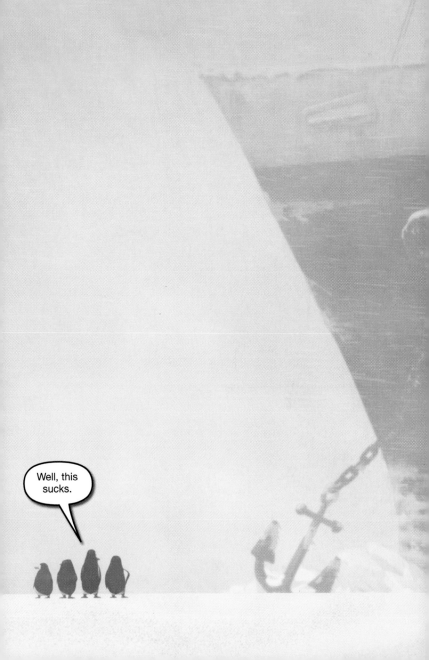

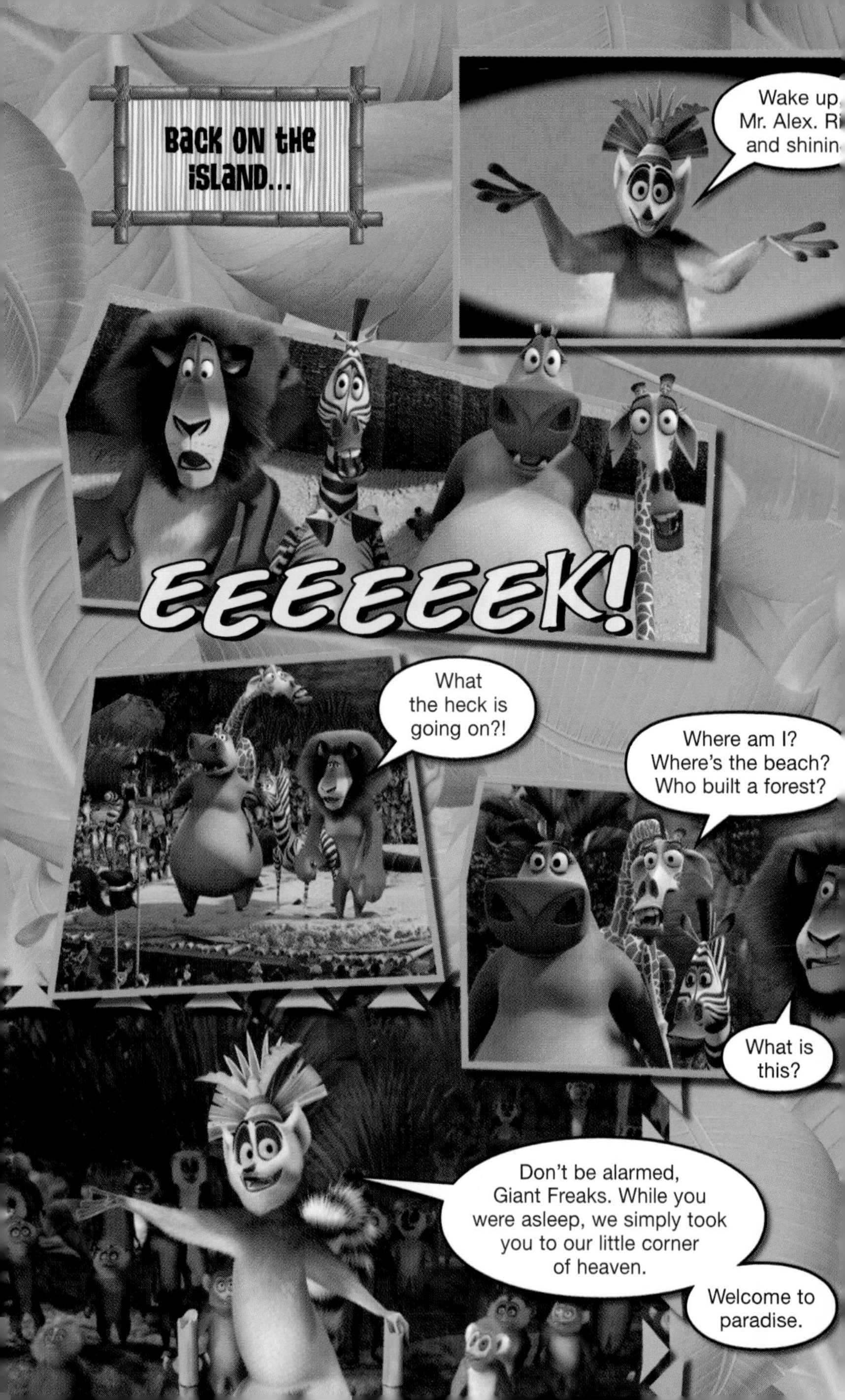

Back on the island...
Wake up, Mr. Alex. Ri and shinin
EEEEEEK!
What the heck is going on?!
Where am I? Where's the beach? Who built a forest?
What is this?
Don't be alarmed, Giant Freaks. While you were asleep, we simply took you to our little corner of heaven.
Welcome to paradise.

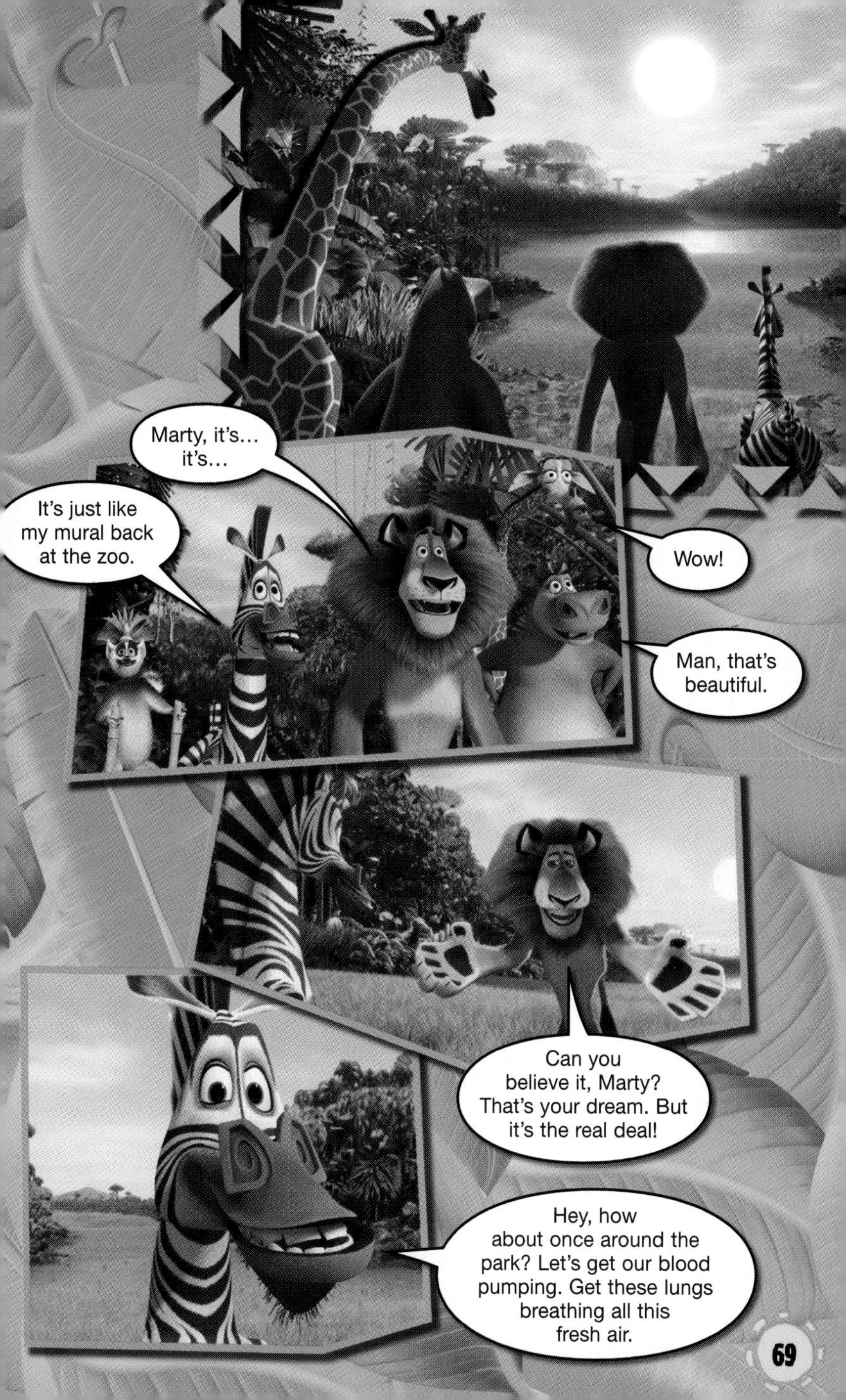
Marty, it's… it's…
It's just like my mural back at the zoo.
Wow!
Man, that's beautiful.
Can you believe it, Marty? That's your dream. But it's the real deal!
Hey, how about once around the park? Let's get our blood pumping. Get these lungs breathing all this fresh air.

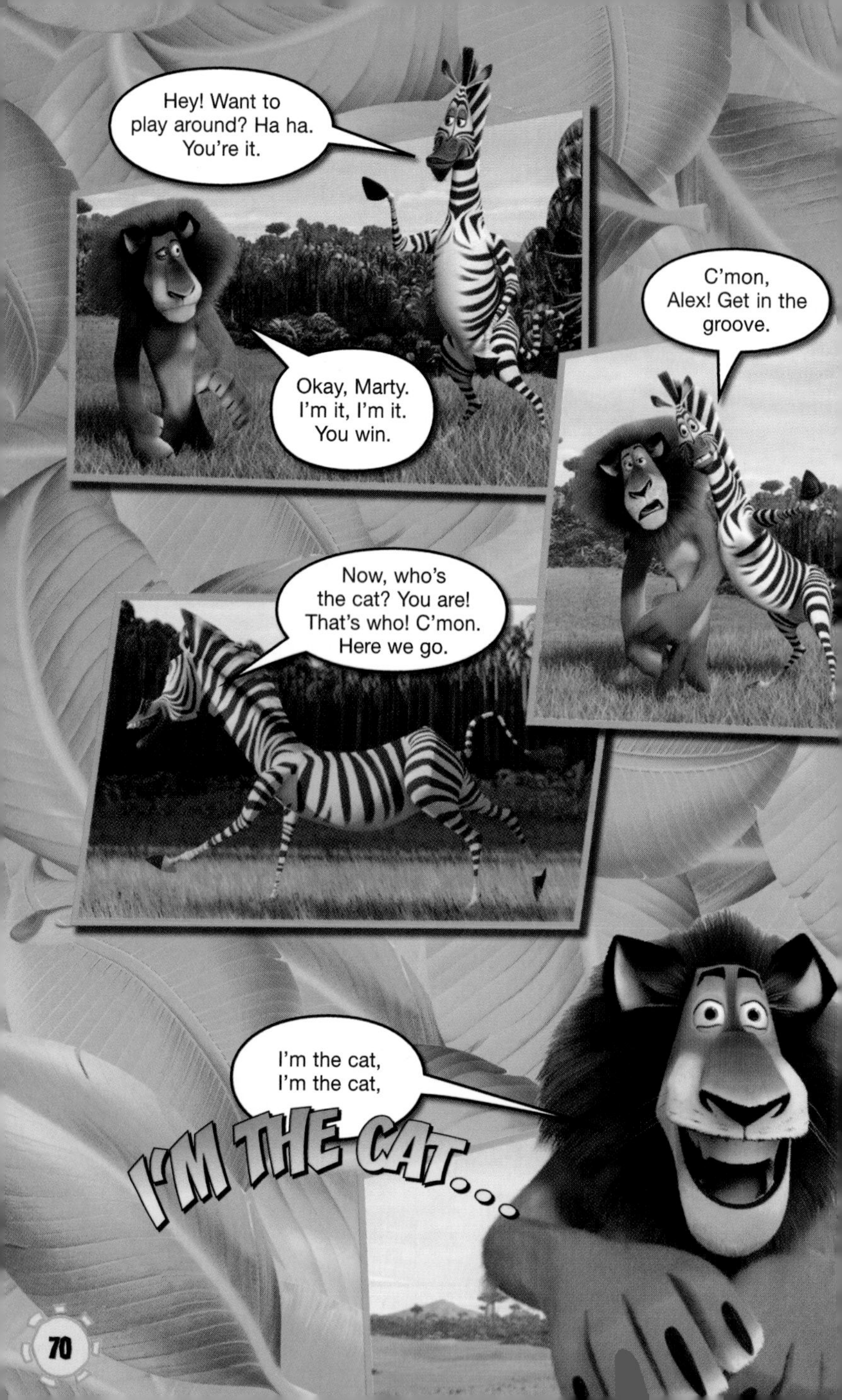
Hey! Want to play around? Ha ha. You're it.
Okay, Marty. I'm it, I'm it. You win.
C'mon, Alex! Get in the groove.
Now, who's the cat? You are! That's who! C'mon. Here we go.
I'm the cat, I'm the cat,
I'M THE CAT...

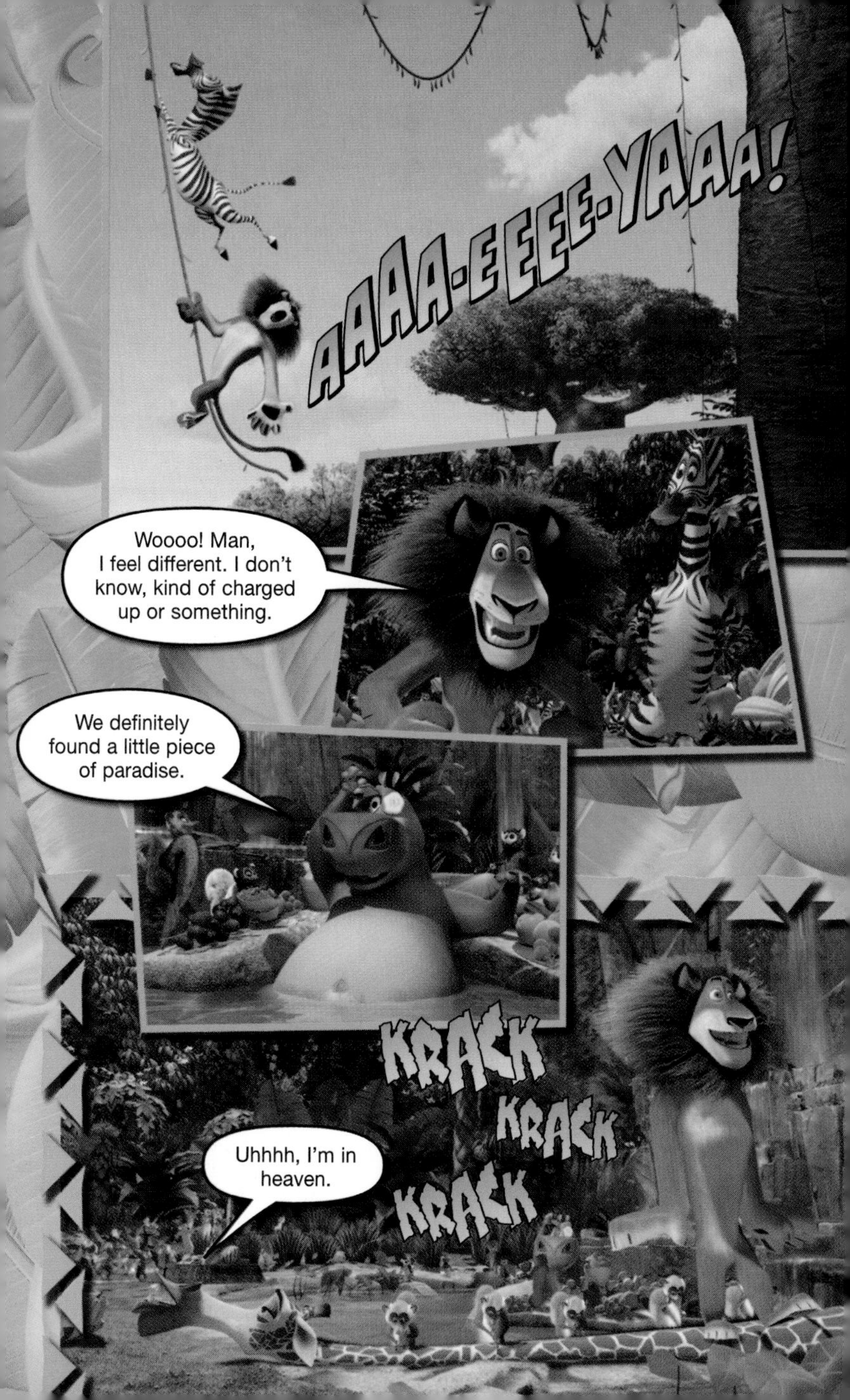
AAAA-EEEE-YAAA!
Woooo! Man, I feel different. I don't know, kind of charged up or something.
We definitely found a little piece of paradise.
KRACK
KRACK
Uhhhh, I'm in heaven.
KRACK

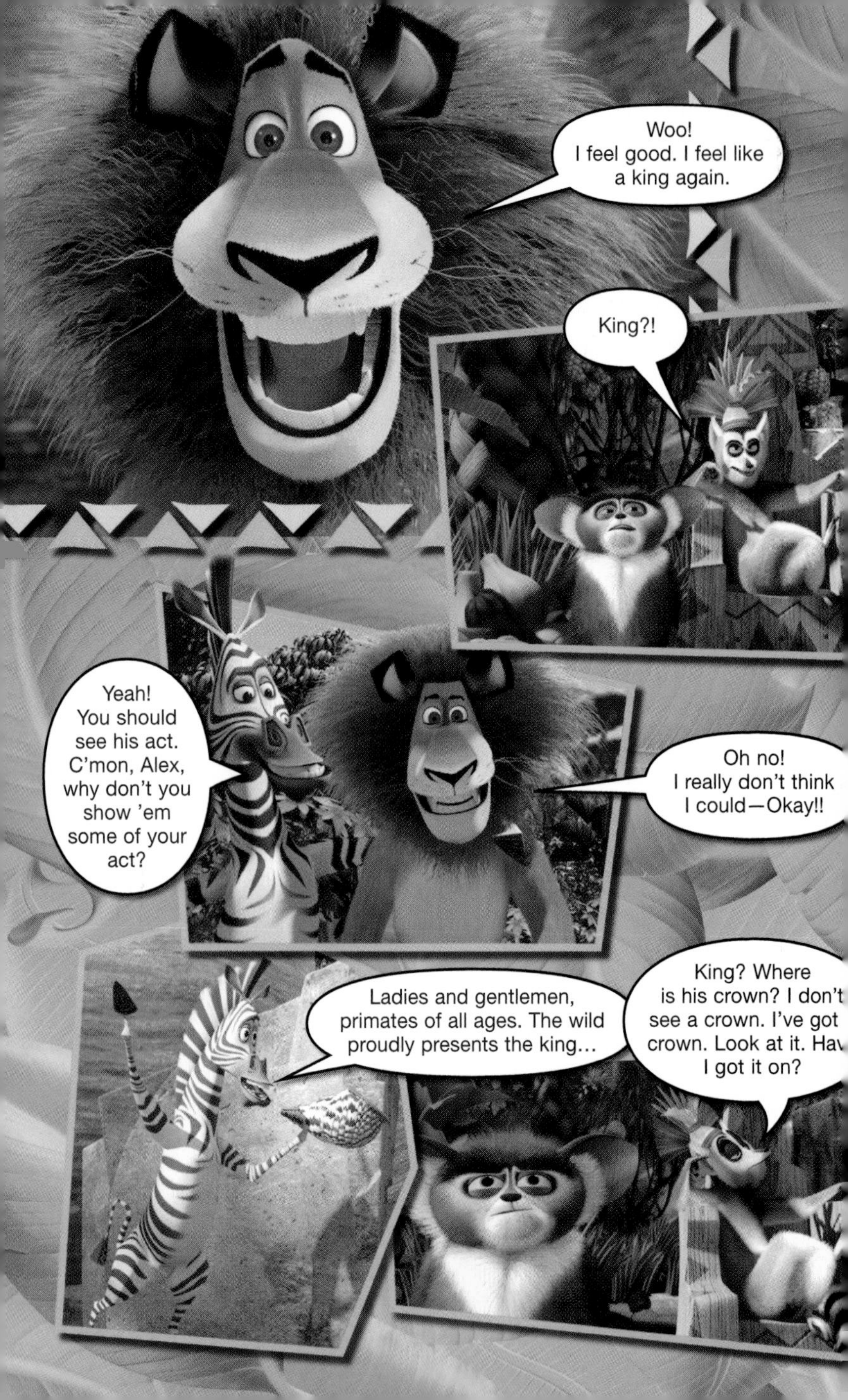
Woo! I feel good. I feel like a king again.
King?!
Yeah! You should see his act. C'mon, Alex, why don't you show 'em some of your act?
Oh no! I really don't think I could—Okay!!
Ladies and gentlemen, primates of all ages. The wild proudly presents the king...
King? Where is his crown? I don't see a crown. I've got crown. Look at it. Hav I got it on?

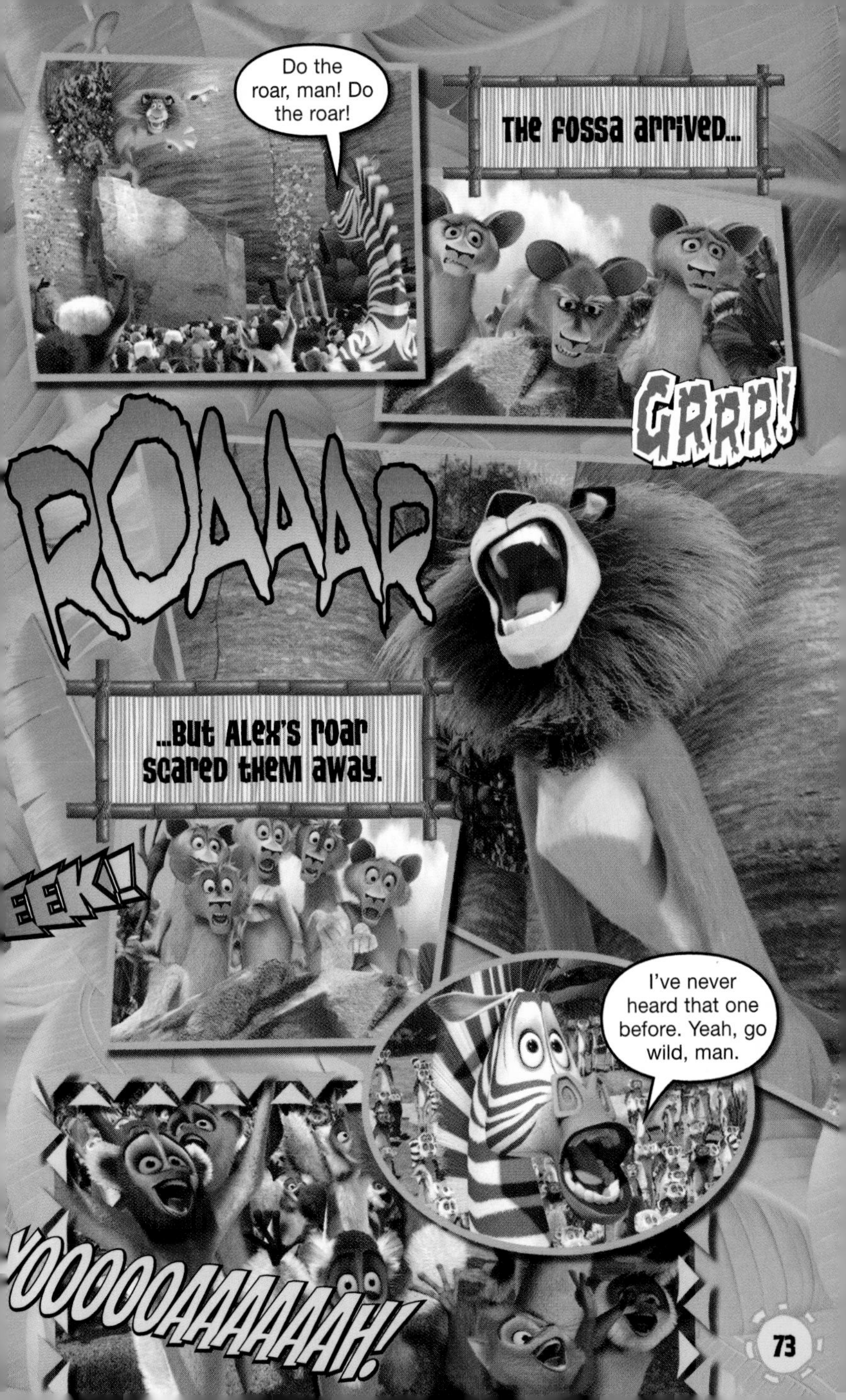
Do the roar, man! Do the roar!
The fossa arrived...
GRRR!
ROAAAR
...But Alex's roar scared them away.
EEK!!
I've never heard that one before. Yeah, go wild, man.
YOOOOOAAAAAAAH!

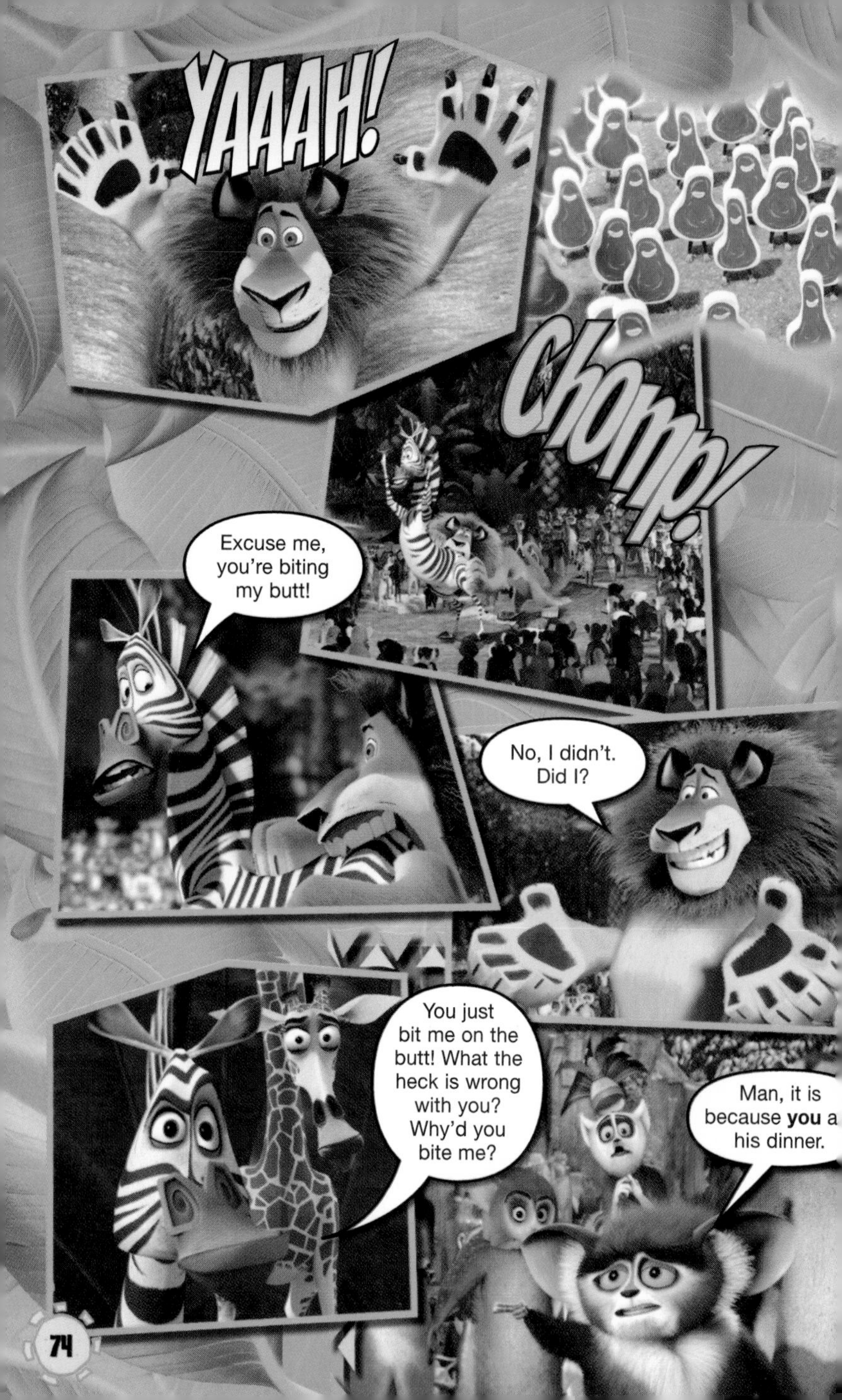

YAAAH!
CHOMP!
Excuse me, you're biting my butt!
No, I didn't. Did I?
You just bit me on the butt! What the heck is wrong with you? Why'd you bite me?
Man, it is because **you** a
his dinner.

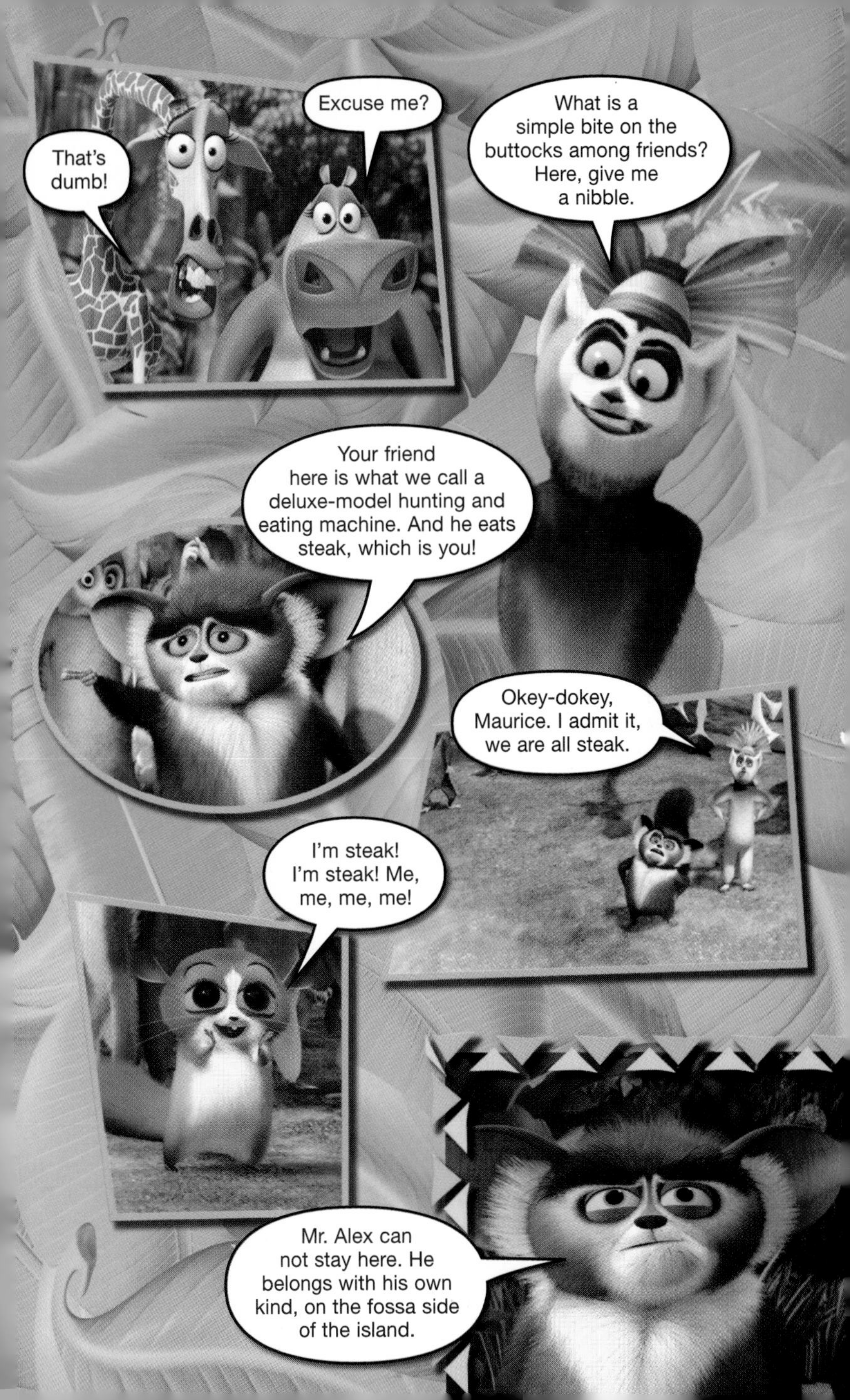
That's dumb!
Excuse me?
What is a simple bite on the buttocks among friends? Here, give me a nibble.
Your friend here is what we call a deluxe-model hunting and eating machine. And he eats steak, which is you!
Okey-dokey, Maurice. I admit it, we are all steak.
I'm steak! I'm steak! Me, me, me, me!
Mr. Alex can not stay here. He belongs with his own kind, on the fossa side of the island.

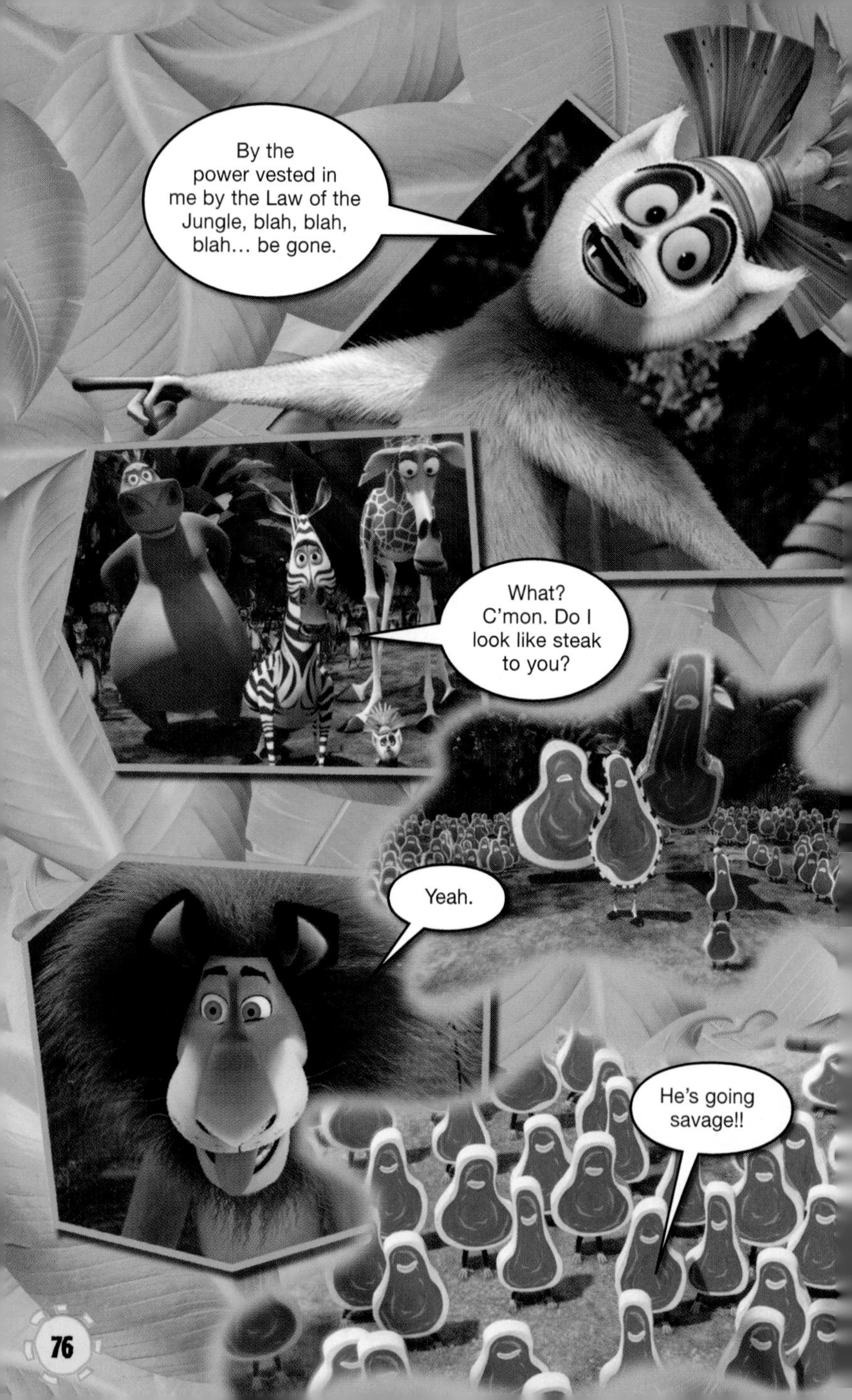
By the power vested in me by the Law of the Jungle, blah, blah, blah… be gone.
What? C'mon. Do I look like steak to you?
Yeah.
He's going savage!!

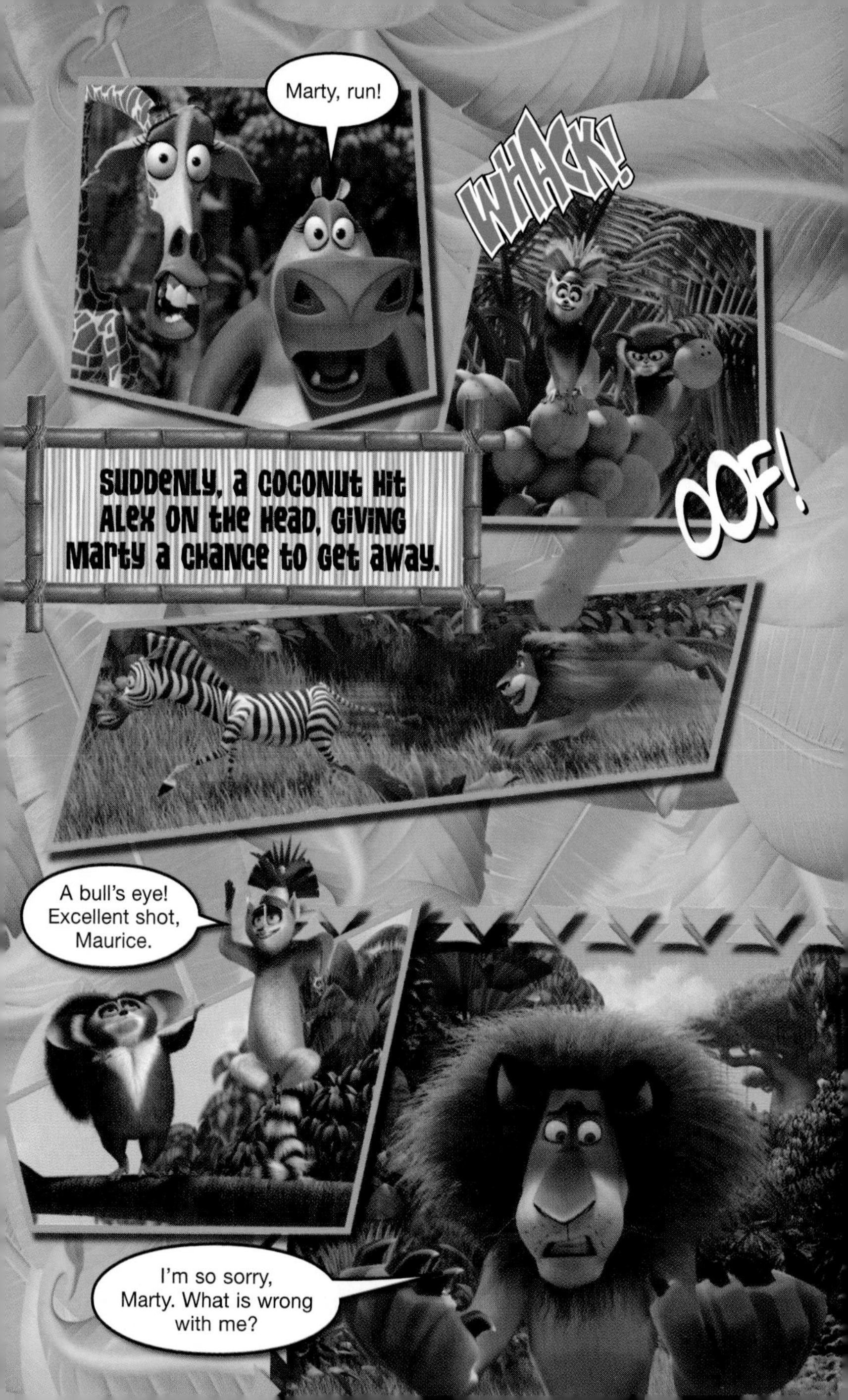
Marty, run!
WHACK!
SUDDENLY, A COCONUT HIT ALEX ON THE HEAD, GIVING MARTY A CHANCE TO GET AWAY.
OOF!
A bull's eye! Excellent shot, Maurice.
I'm so sorry, Marty. What is wrong with me?

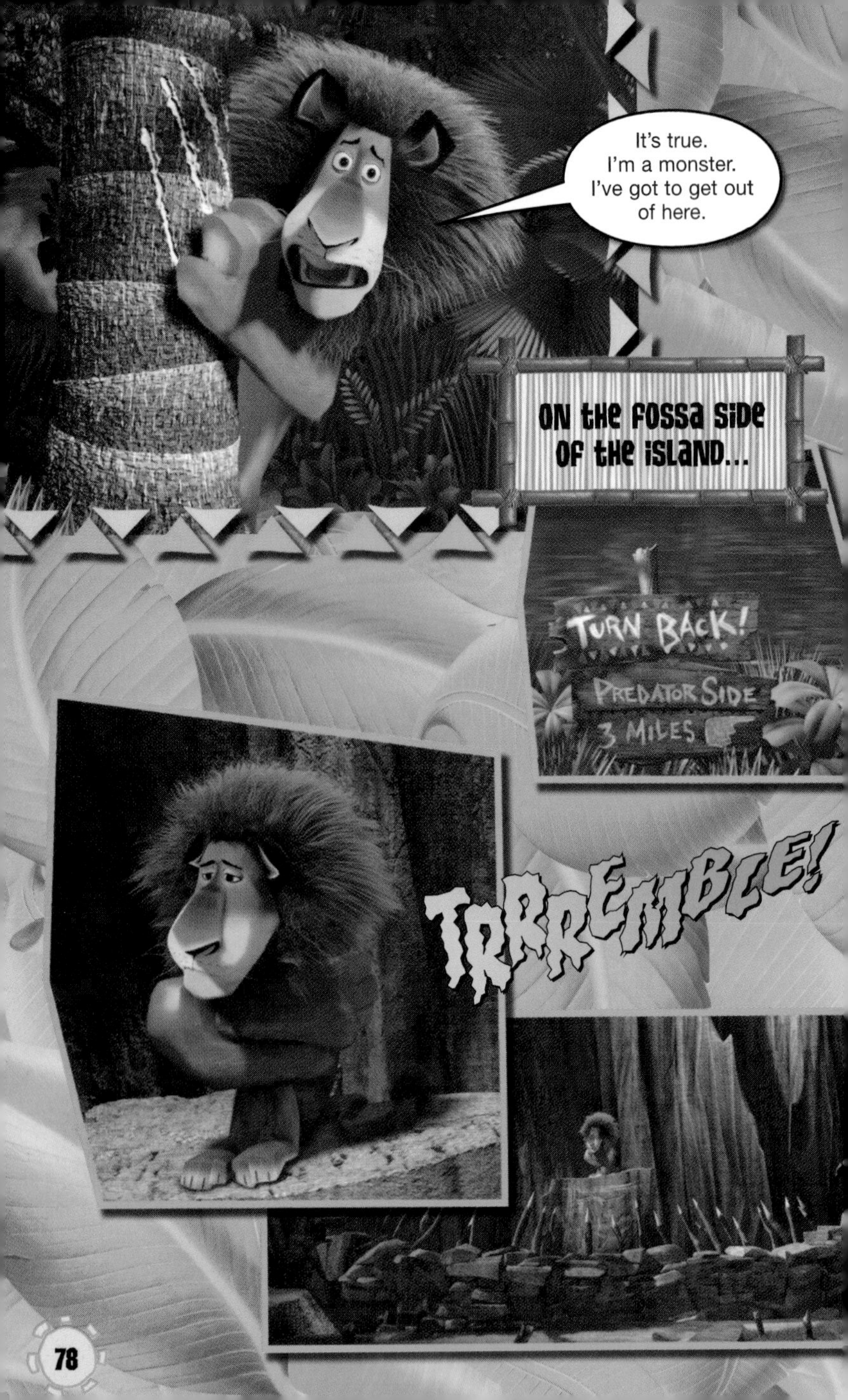
It's true. I'm a monster. I've got to get out of here.
ON THE FOSSA SIDE OF THE ISLAND...
TURN BACK!
PREDATOR SIDE
3 MILES
TRRREMBLE!

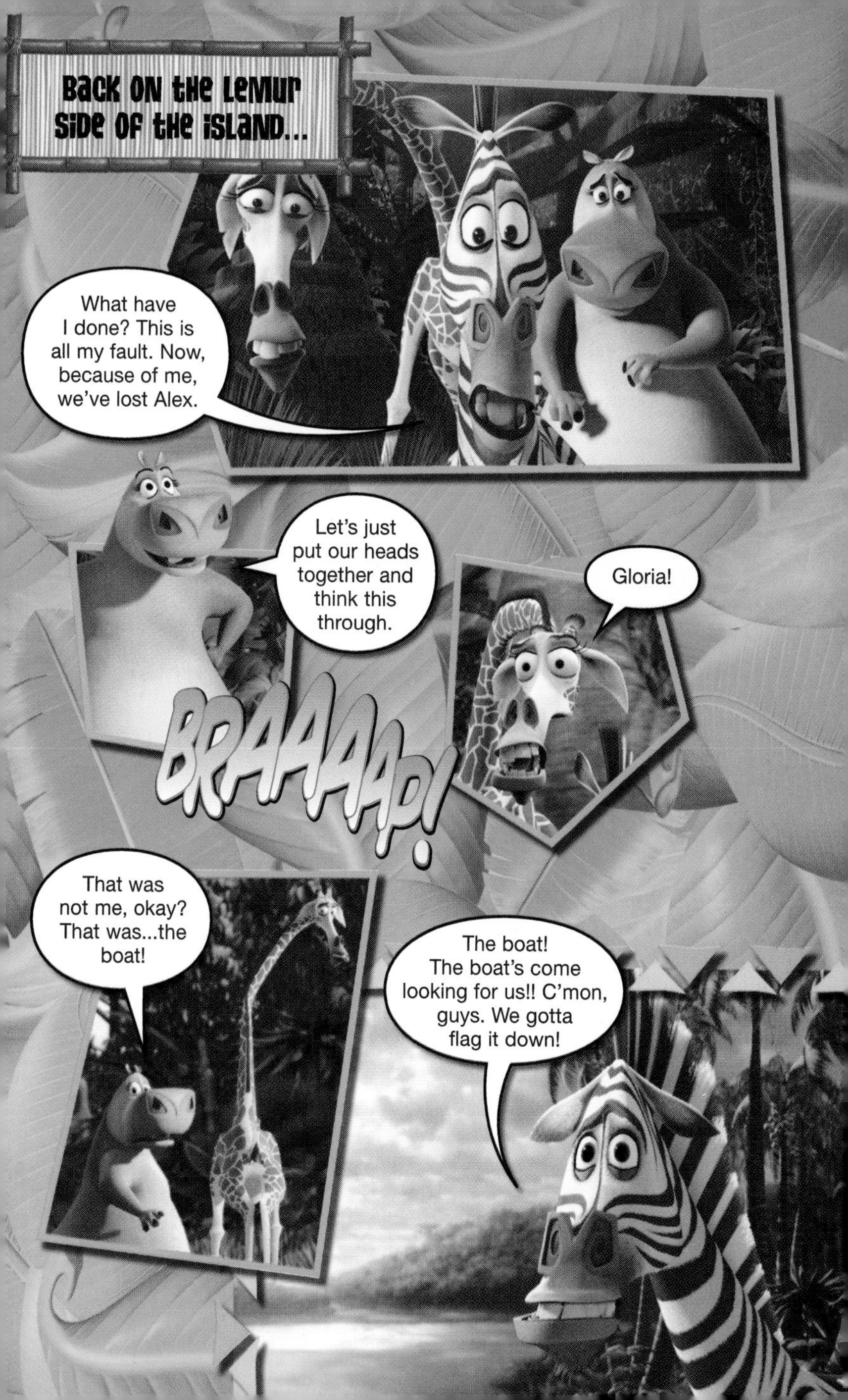
Back on the Lemur side of the island...
What have I done? This is all my fault. Now, because of me, we've lost Alex.
Let's just put our heads together and think this through.
Gloria!
BRAAAAAP!
That was not me, okay? That was...the boat!
The boat! The boat's come looking for us!! C'mon, guys. We gotta flag it down!

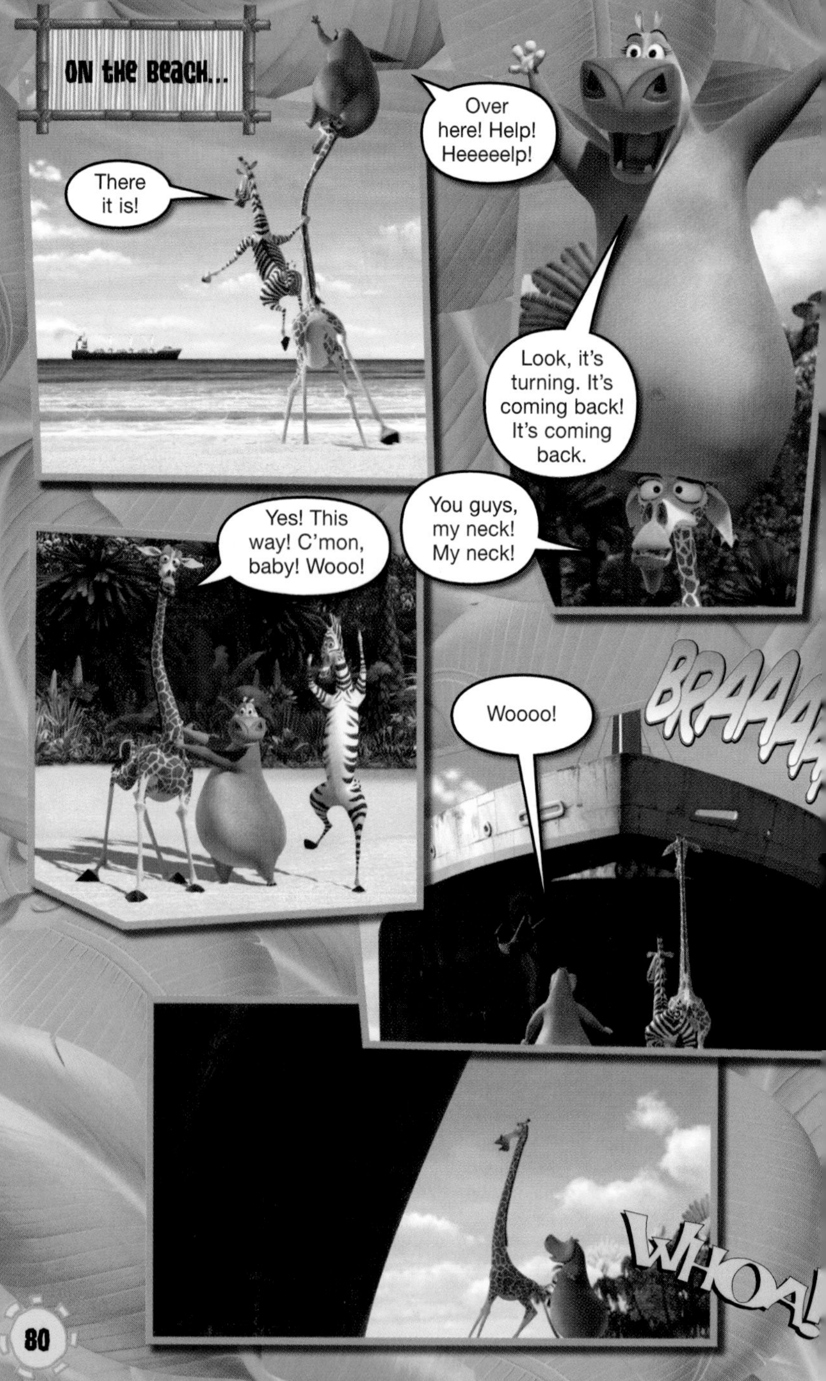
ON THE BEACH...
There it is!
Over here! Help! Heeeeelp!
Look, it's turning. It's coming back! It's coming back.
Yes! This way! C'mon, baby! Wooo!
You guys, my neck! My neck!
Woooo!
WHOA!

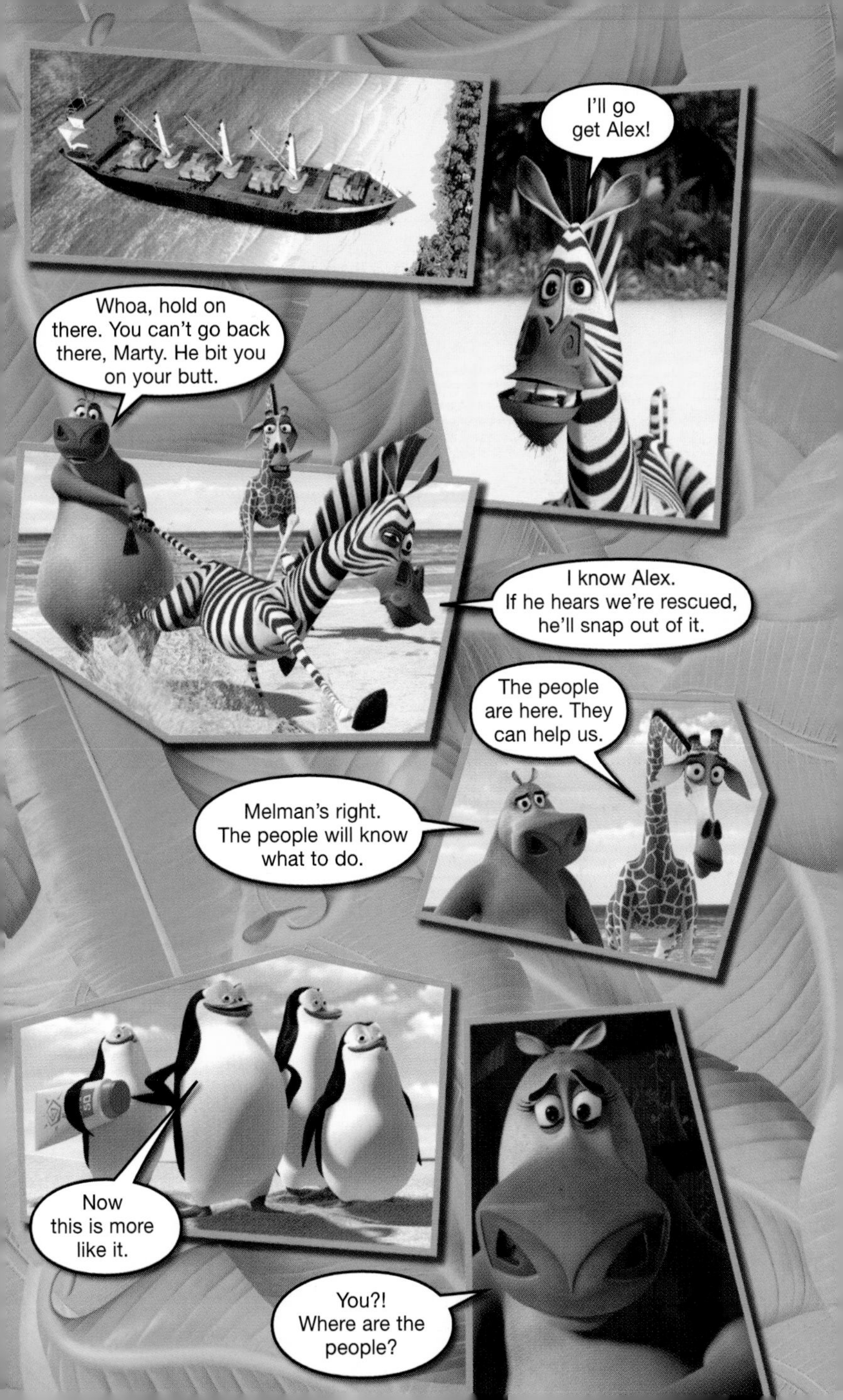
I'll go get Alex!
Whoa, hold on there. You can't go back there, Marty. He bit you on your butt.
I know Alex. If he hears we're rescued, he'll snap out of it.
The people are here. They can help us.
Melman's right. The people will know what to do.
Now this is more like it.
You?! Where are the people?

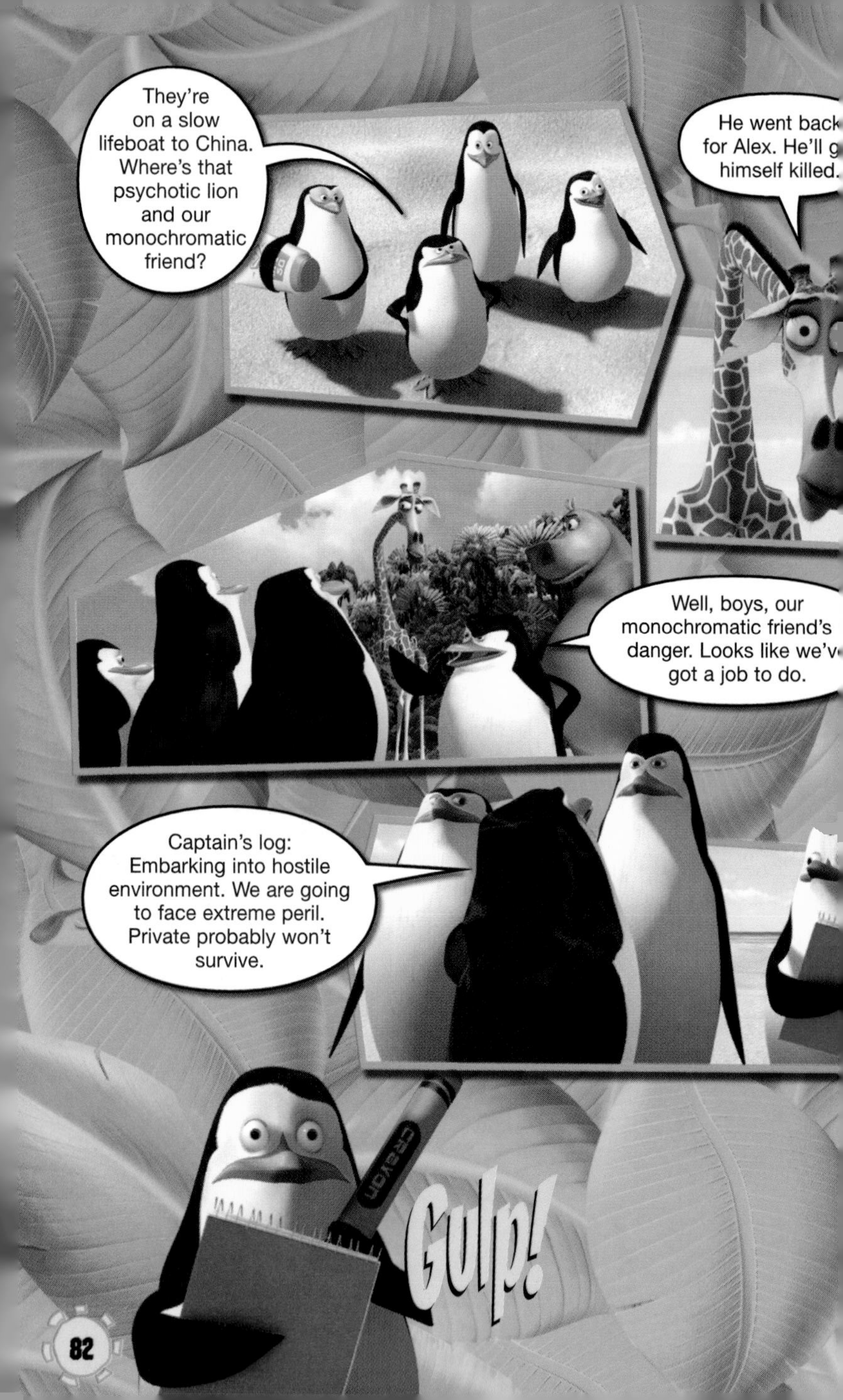
They're on a slow lifeboat to China. Where's that psychotic lion and our monochromatic friend?
He went back for Alex. He'll g himself killed.
Well, boys, our monochromatic friend's danger. Looks like we'v got a job to do.
Captain's log: Embarking into hostile environment. We are going to face extreme peril. Private probably won't survive.
Crayon
Gulp!

Back on the fossa side...

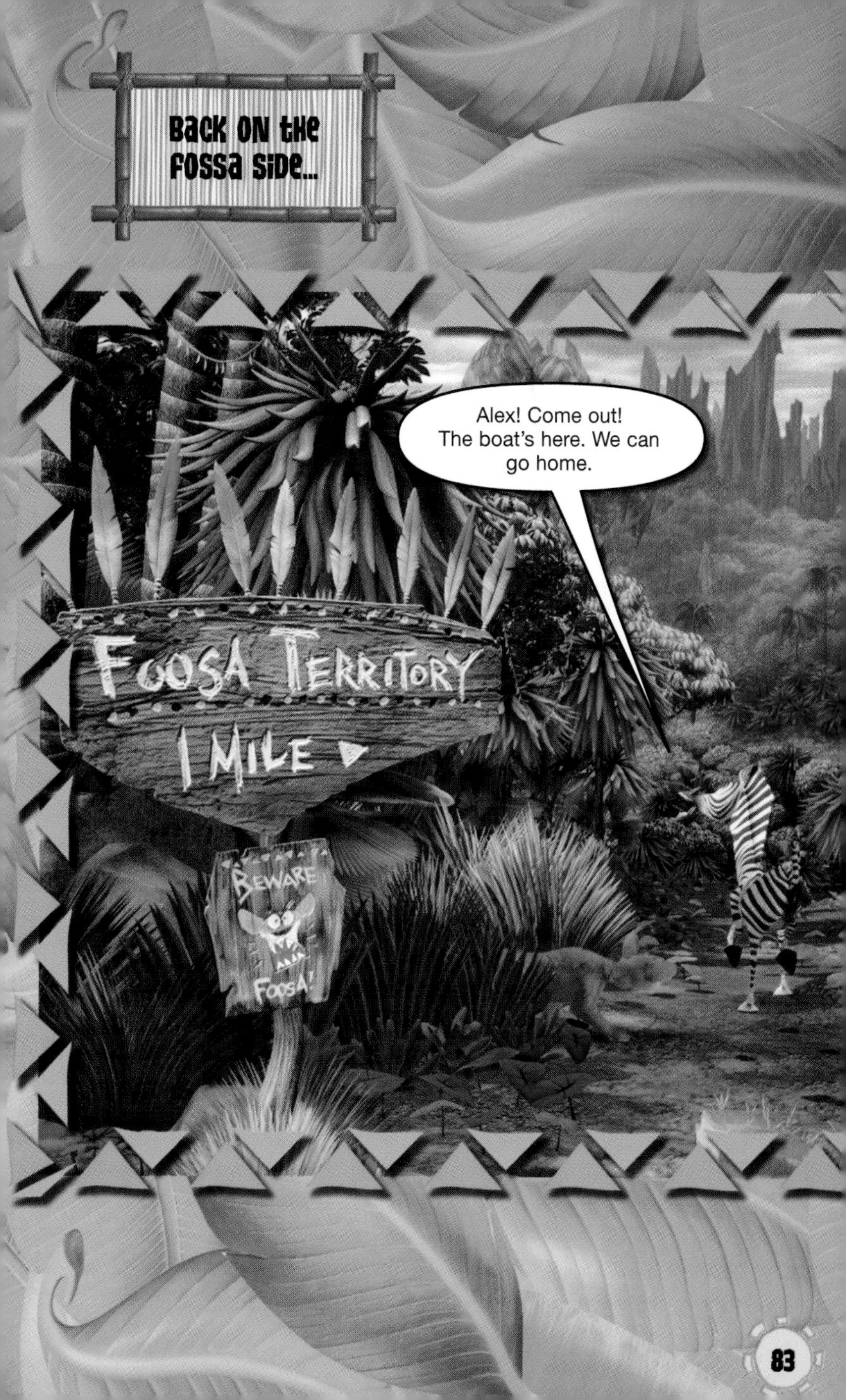
Alex! Come out! The boat's here. We can go home.
Foosa Territory
1 Mile
Beware
Foosa!

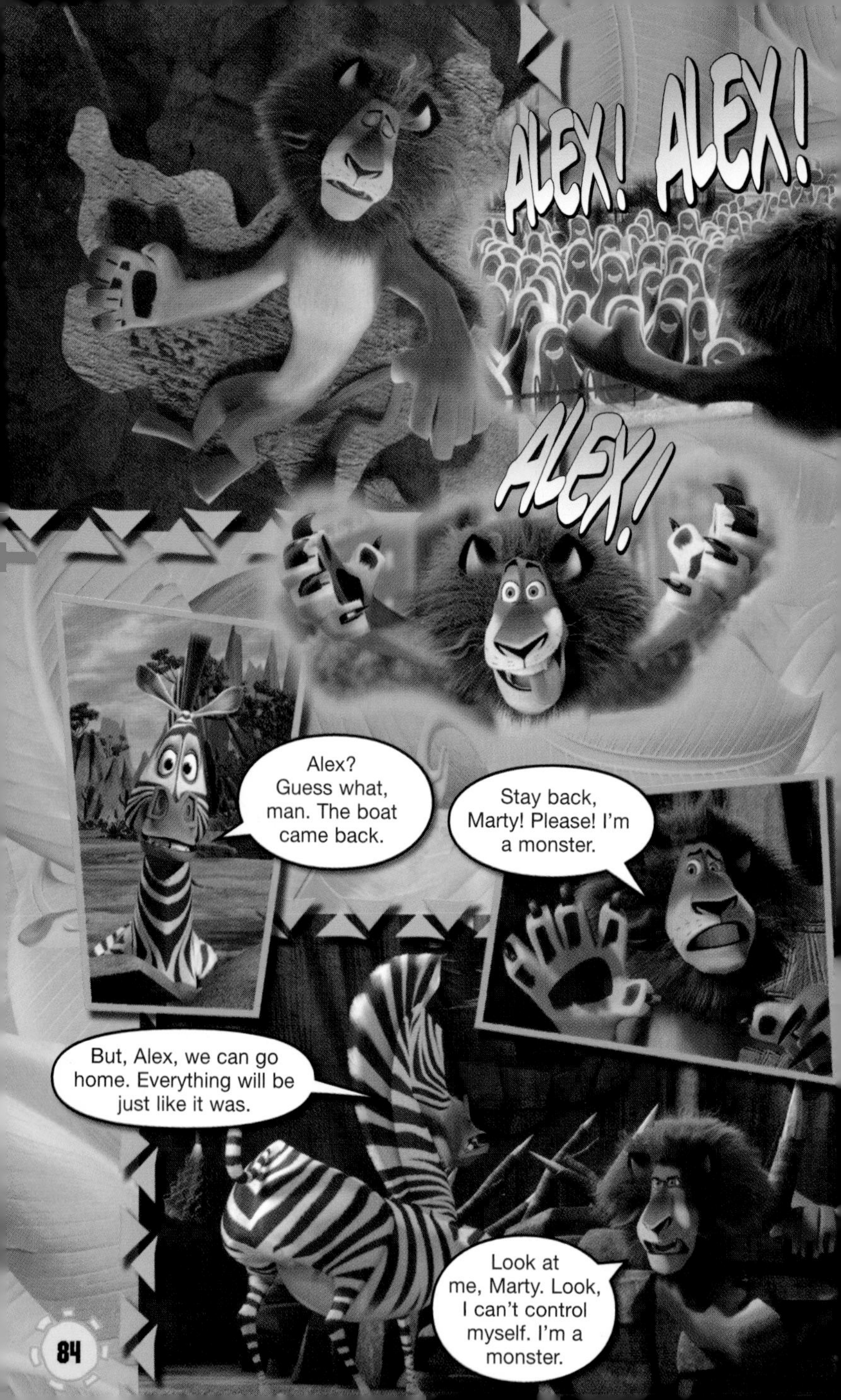

ALEX! ALEX!
ALEX!
Alex? Guess what, man. The boat came back.
Stay back, Marty! Please! I'm a monster.
But, Alex, we can go home. Everything will be just like it was.
Look at me, Marty. Look, I can't control myself. I'm a monster.

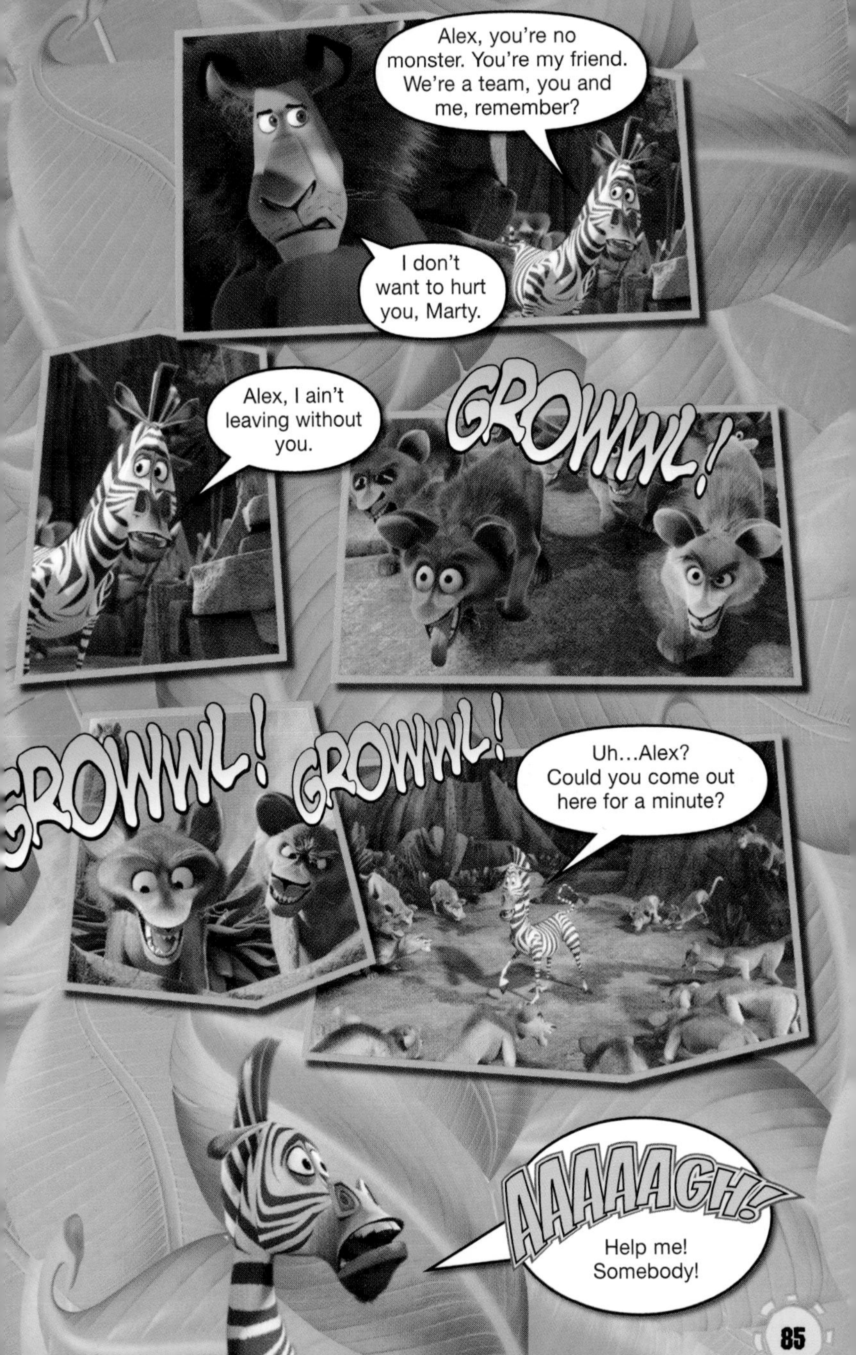
Alex, you're no monster. You're my friend. We're a team, you and me, remember?
I don't want to hurt you, Marty.
Alex, I ain't leaving without you.
GROWWL!
GROWWL!
GROWWL!
Uh…Alex? Could you come out here for a minute?
AAAAAGH!
Help me! Somebody!

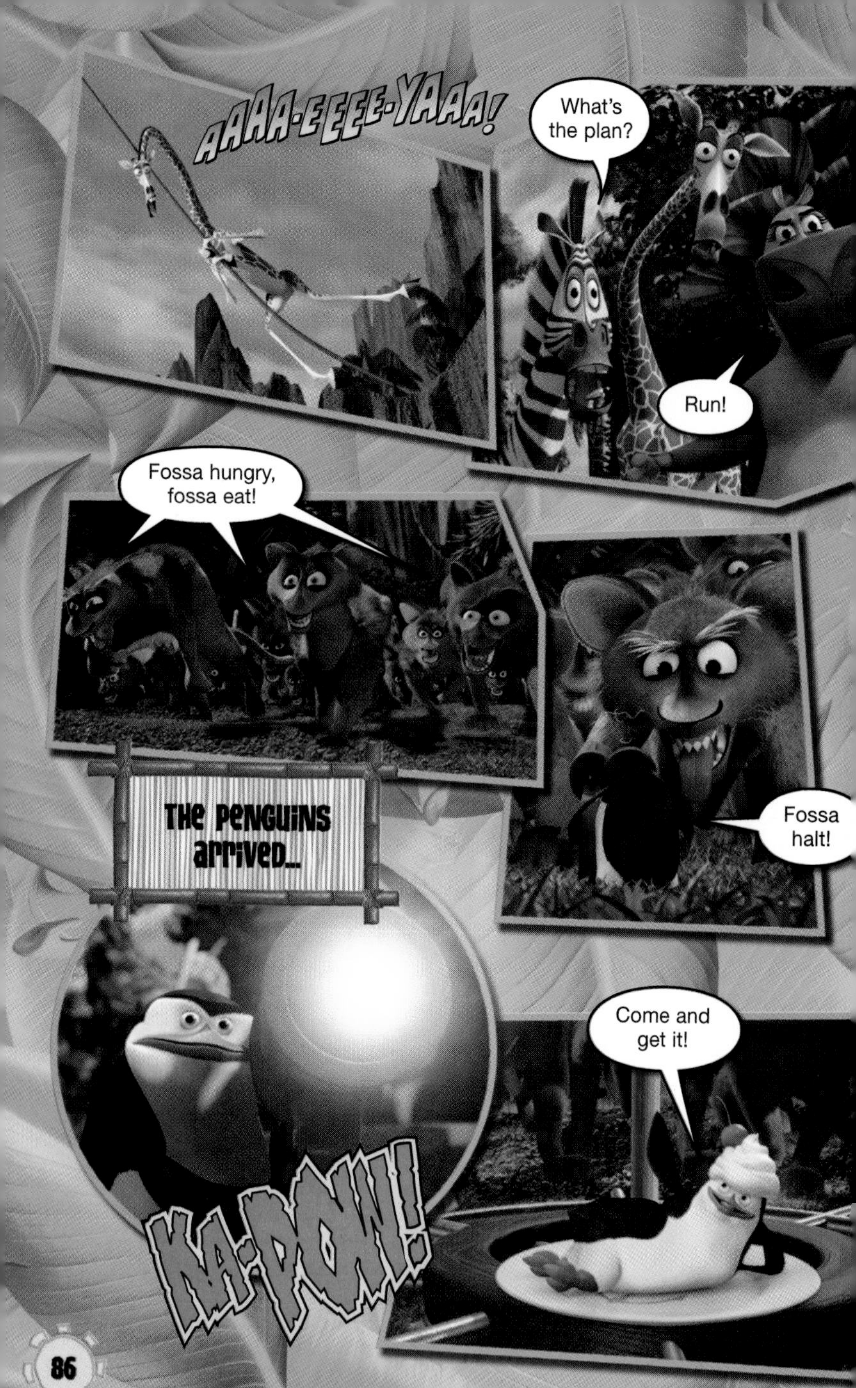
AAAA-EEEE-YAAAA!
What's the plan?
Run!
Fossa hungry, fossa eat!
Fossa halt!
The penguins arrived...
Come and get it!
KA-POW!

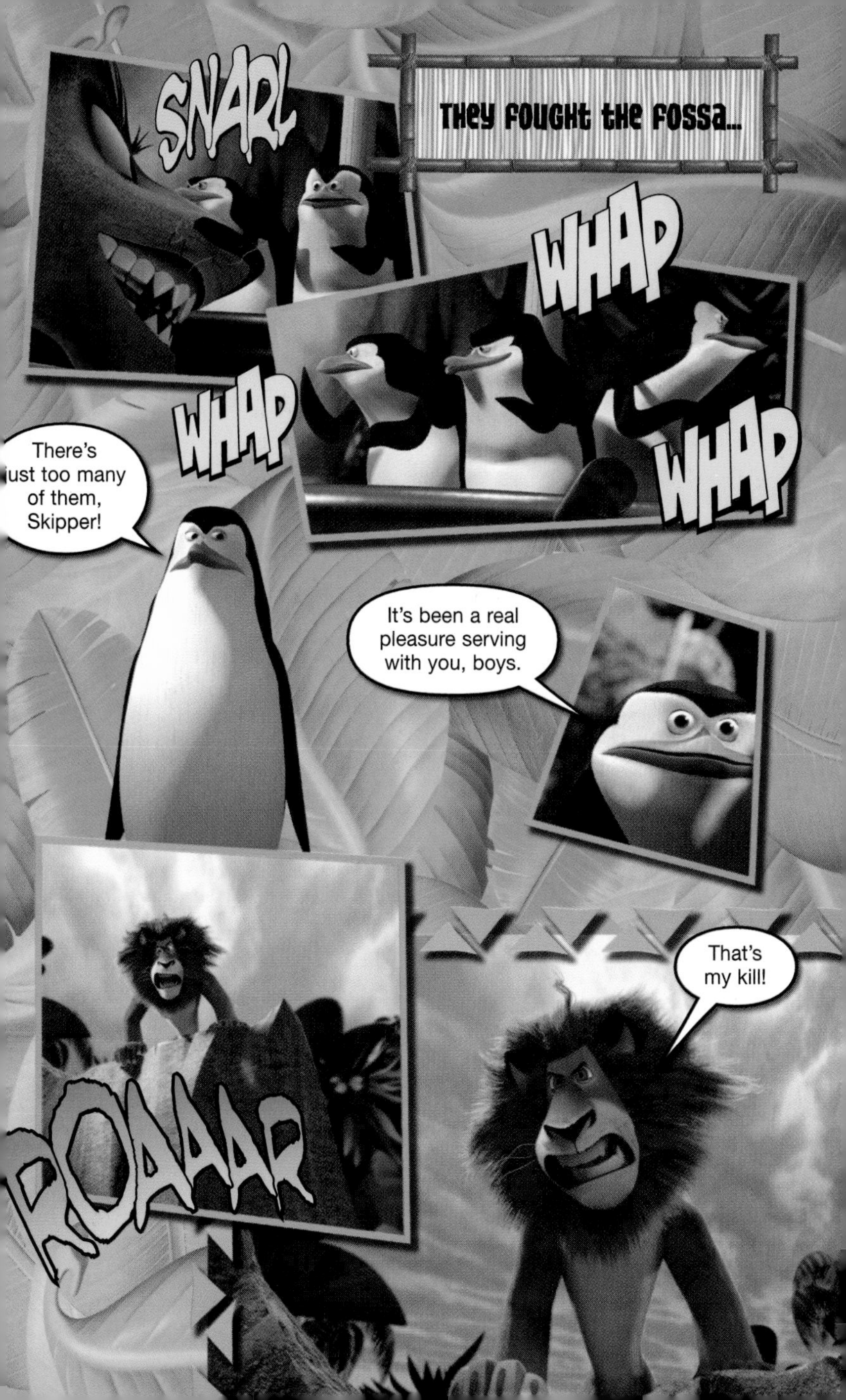
SNARL
They fought the fossa...
WHAP
WHAP
WHAP
There's just too many of them, Skipper!
It's been a real pleasure serving with you, boys.
ROAAAR
That's my kill!

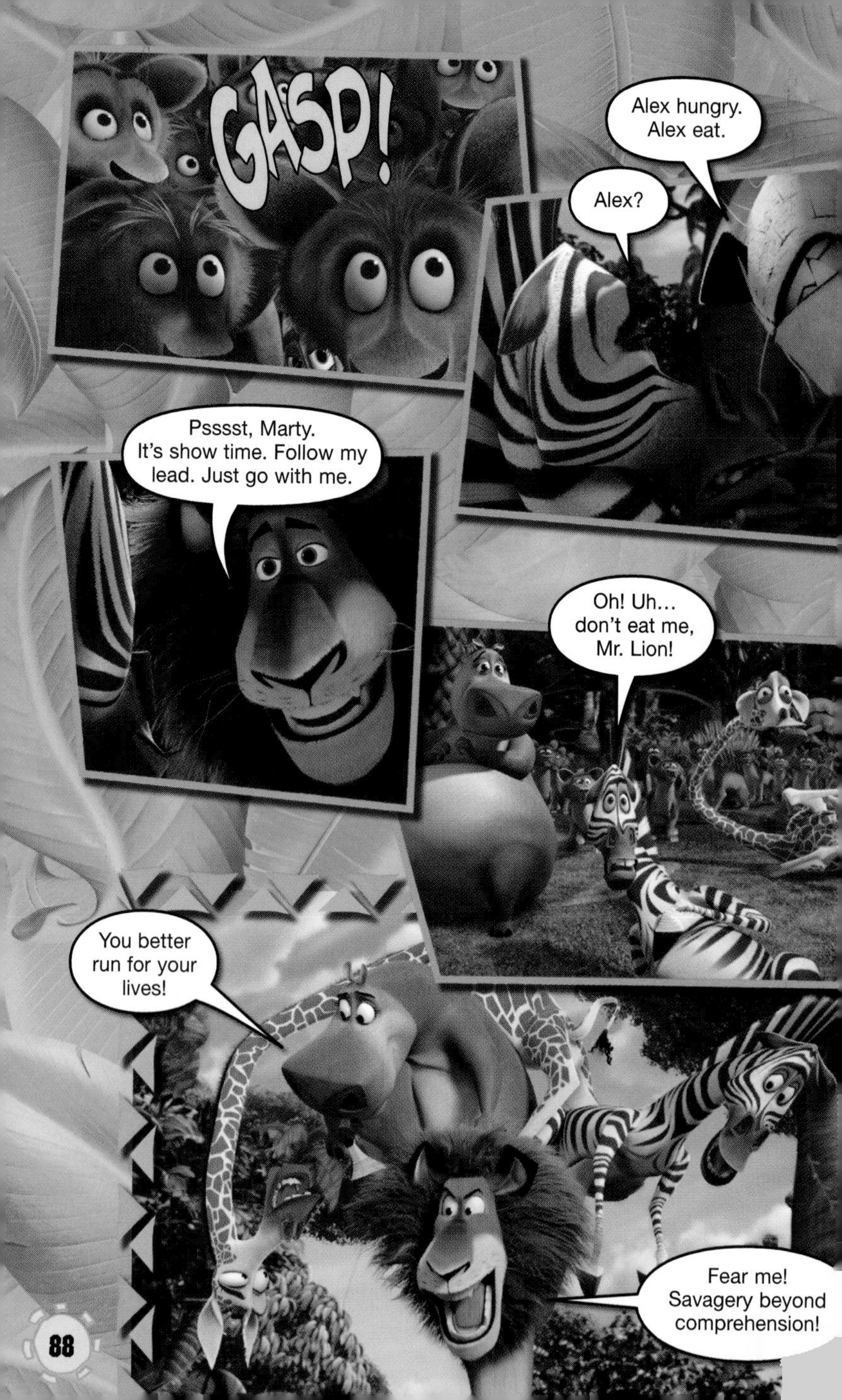
GASP!
Alex hungry. Alex eat.
Alex?
Psssst, Marty. It's show time. Follow my lead. Just go with me.
Oh! Uh... don't eat me, Mr. Lion!
You better run for your lives!
Fear me! Savagery beyond comprehension!

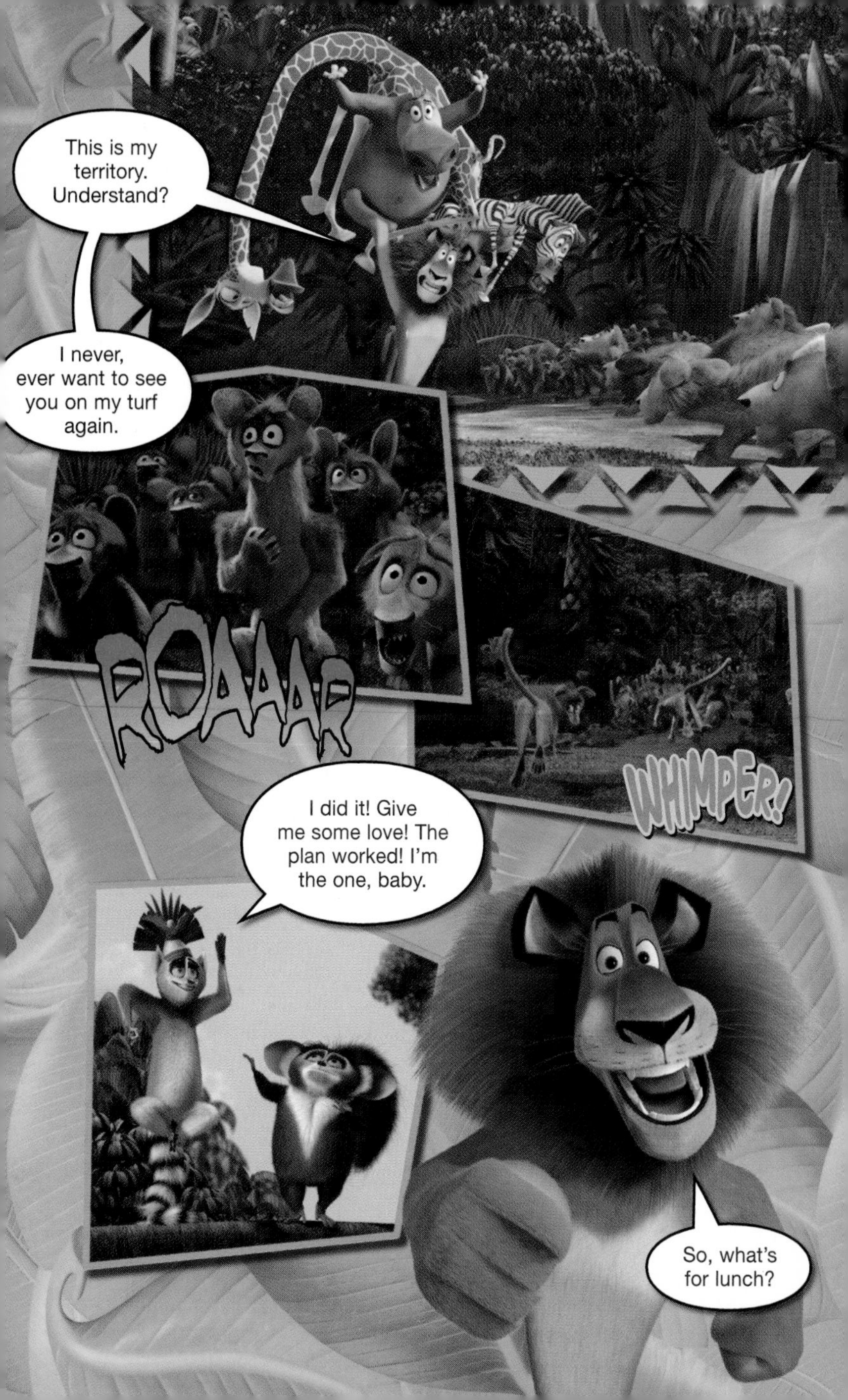
This is my territory. Understand?
I never, ever want to see you on my turf again.
ROAAAR
WHIMPER!
I did it! Give me some love! The plan worked! I'm the one, baby.
So, what's for lunch?

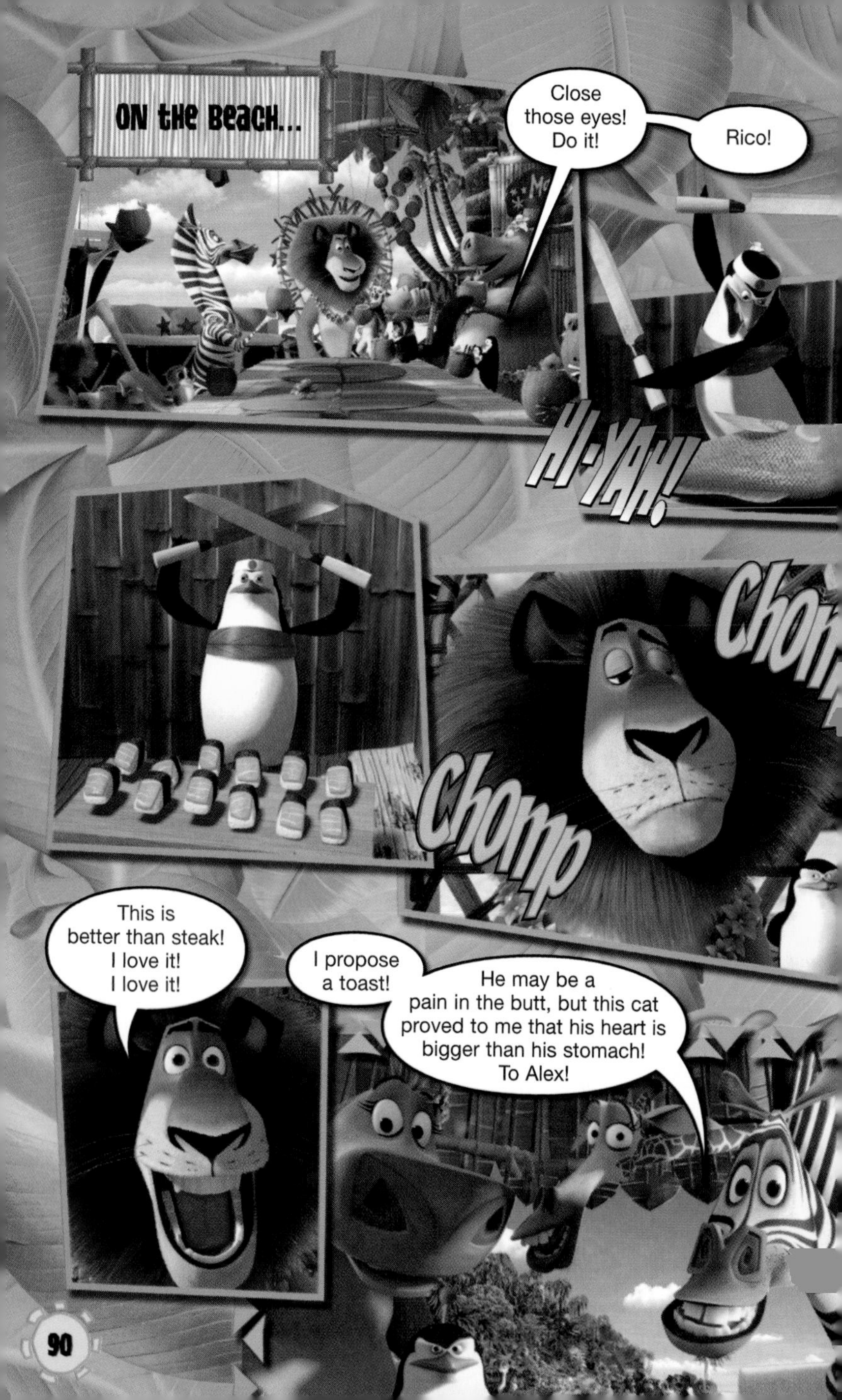
ON THE BEACH...
Close those eyes! Do it!
Rico!
HI-YAH!
Chomp
Chomp
This is better than steak! I love it! I love it!
I propose a toast!
He may be a pain in the butt, but this cat proved to me that his heart is bigger than his stomach! To Alex!

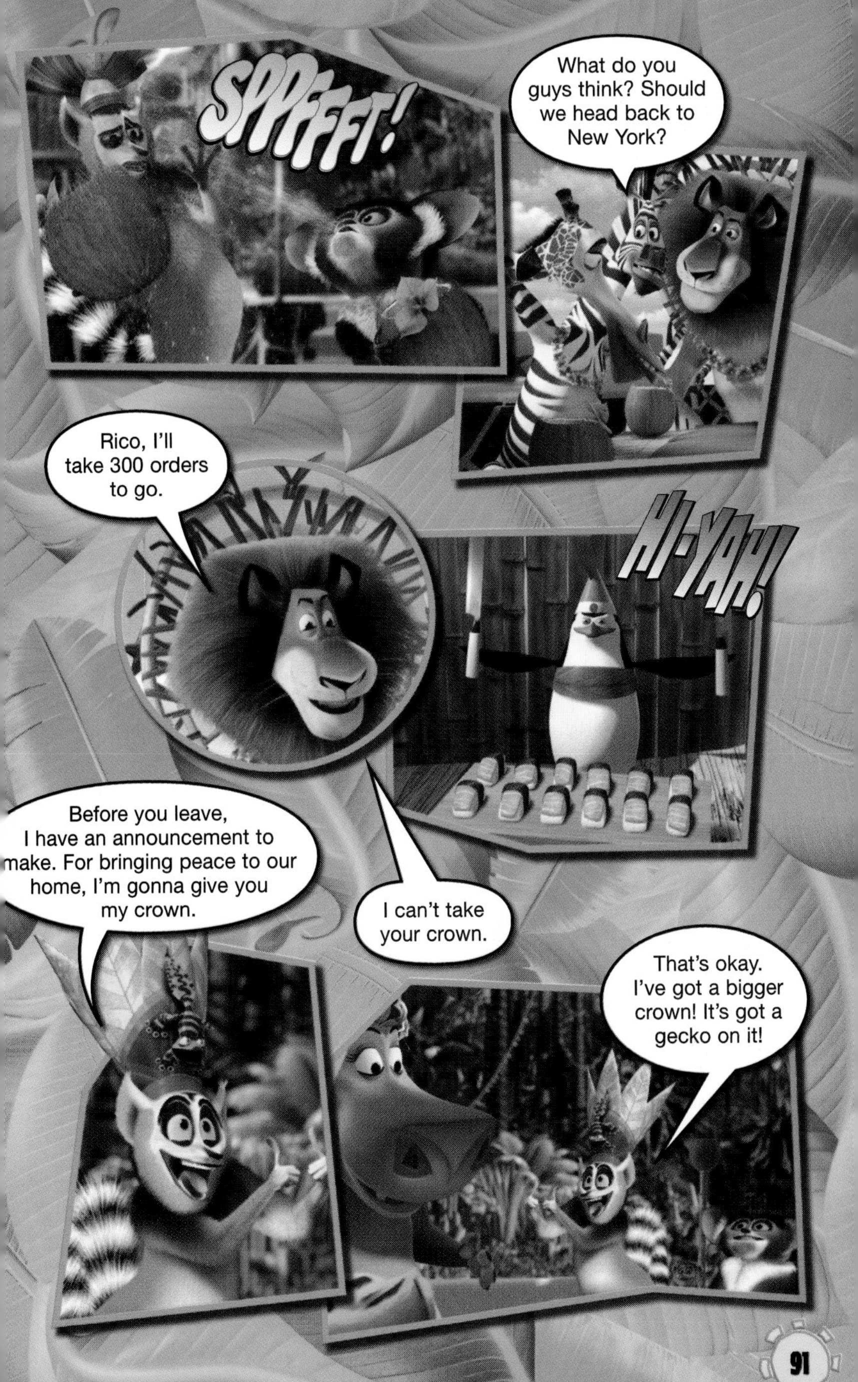
SPPFFFT!
What do you guys think? Should we head back to New York?
Rico, I'll take 300 orders to go.
HI-YAH!
Before you leave, I have an announcement to make. For bringing peace to our home, I'm gonna give you my crown.
I can't take your crown.
That's okay. I've got a bigger crown! It's got a gecko on it!

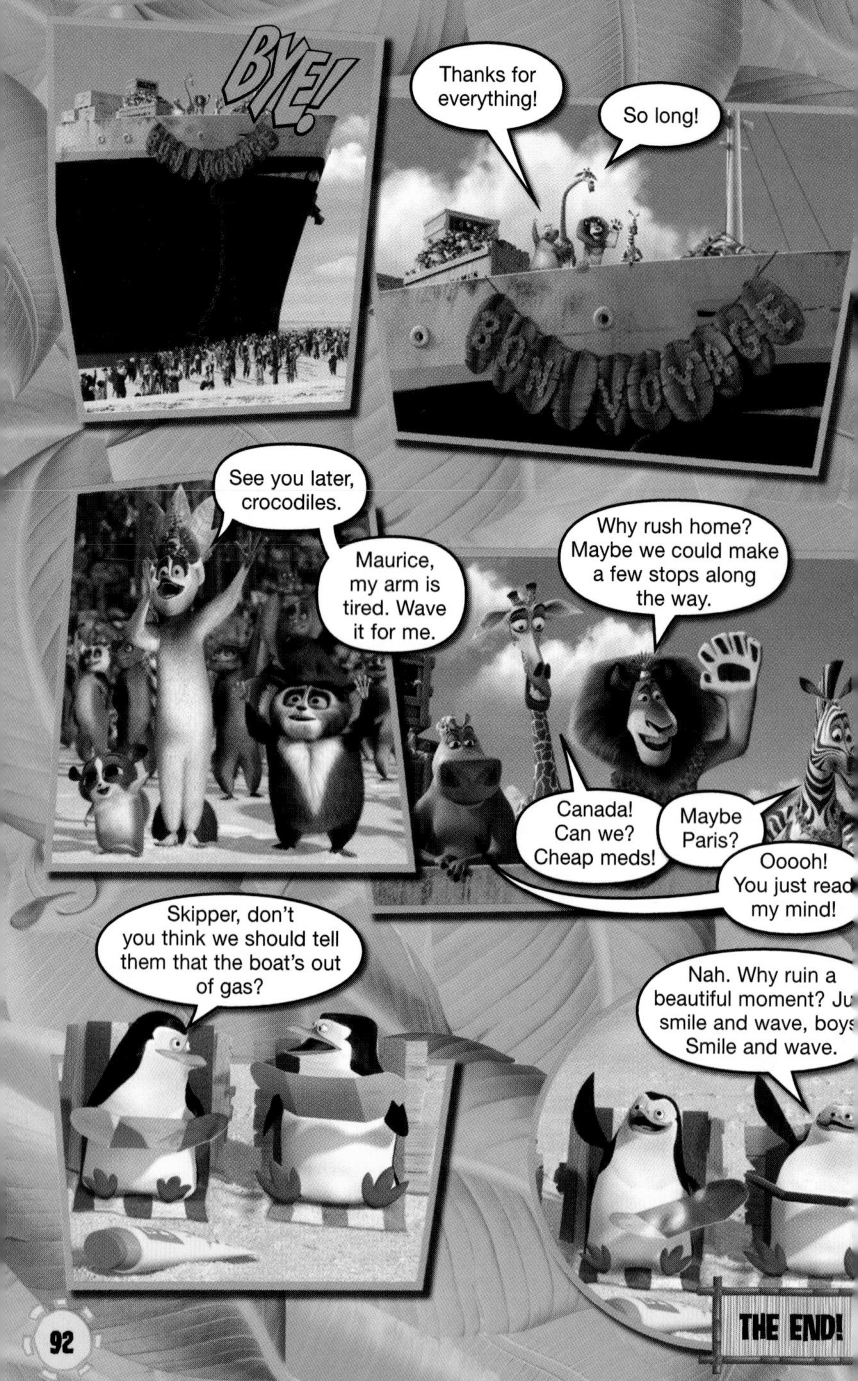
BYE!
BON VOYAGE
Thanks for everything!
So long!
BON VOYAGE
See you later, crocodiles.
Maurice, my arm is tired. Wave it for me.
Why rush home? Maybe we could make a few stops along the way.
Canada! Can we? Cheap meds!
Maybe Paris?
Ooooh! You just read my mind!
Skipper, don't you think we should tell them that the boat's out of gas?
Nah. Why ruin a beautiful moment? Ju
smile and wave, boy
Smile and wave.
THE END!

MANGA

.HACK//LEGEND OF THE TWILIGHT
ALICHINO
ANGELIC LAYER
BABY BIRTH
BRAIN POWERED
BRIGADOON
B'TX
CANDIDATE FOR GODDESS, THE
CARDCAPTOR SAKURA
CARDCAPTOR SAKURA - MASTER OF THE CLOW
CHRONICLES OF THE CURSED SWORD
CLAMP SCHOOL DETECTIVES
CLOVER
COMIC PARTY
CORRECTOR YUI
COWBOY BEBOP
COWBOY BEBOP: SHOOTING STAR
CRESCENT MOON
CROSS
CULDCEPT
CYBORG 009
D•N•ANGEL
DEARS
DEMON DIARY
DEMON ORORON, THE
DIGIMON
DIGIMON TAMERS
DIGIMON ZERO TWO
DRAGON HUNTER
DRAGON KNIGHTS
DRAGON VOICE
DREAM SAGA
DUKLYON: CLAMP SCHOOL DEFENDERS
ET CETERA
ETERNITY
FAERIES' LANDING
FLCL
FLOWER OF THE DEEP SLEEP
FORBIDDEN DANCE
FRUITS BASKET
G GUNDAM
GATEKEEPERS
GIRL GOT GAME
GUNDAM SEED ASTRAY
GUNDAM WING
GUNDAM WING: BATTLEFIELD OF PACIFISTS
GUNDAM WING: ENDLESS WALTZ
GUNDAM WING: THE LAST OUTPOST (G-UNIT)
HANDS OFF!

HARLEM BEAT
HYPER RUNE
I.N.V.U.
INITIAL D
INSTANT TEEN: JUST ADD NUTS
JING: KING OF BANDITS
JING: KING OF BANDITS - TWILIGHT TALES
JULINE
KARE KANO
KILL ME, KISS ME
KINDAICHI CASE FILES, THE
KING OF HELL
KODOCHA: SANA'S STAGE
LEGEND OF CHUN HYANG, THE
LOVE OR MONEY
MAGIC KNIGHT RAYEARTH I
MAGIC KNIGHT RAYEARTH II
MAN OF MANY FACES
MARMALADE BOY
MARS
MARS: HORSE WITH NO NAME
MINK
MIRACLE GIRLS
MODEL
MOURYOU KIDEN: LEGEND OF THE NYMPH
NECK AND NECK
ONE
ONE I LOVE, THE
PEACH FUZZ
PEACH GIRL
PEACH GIRL: CHANGE OF HEART
PITA-TEN
PLANET LADDER
PLANETES
PRESIDENT DAD
PRINCESS AI
PSYCHIC ACADEMY
QUEEN'S KNIGHT, THE
RAGNAROK
RAVE MASTER
REALITY CHECK
REBIRTH
REBOUND
RISING STARS OF MANGA
SAILOR MOON
SAINT TAIL
SAMURAI GIRL REAL BOUT HIGH SCHOOL
SEIKAI TRILOGY, THE
SGT. FROG
SHAOLIN SISTERS

ALSO AVAILABLE FROM  TOKYOPOP®

SHIRAHIME-SYO: SNOW GODDESS TALES
SHUTTERBOX
SKULL MAN, THE
SUIKODEN III
SUKI
TAROT CAFÉ, THE
THREADS OF TIME
TOKYO BABYLON
TOKYO MEW MEW
VAMPIRE GAME
WARCRAFT
WISH
WORLD OF HARTZ
ZODIAC P.I.

CINE-MANGA®

ALADDIN
CARDCAPTORS
DUEL MASTERS
FAIRLY ODDPARENTS, THE
FAMILY GUY
FINDING NEMO
G.I. JOE SPY TROOPS
GREATEST STARS OF THE NBA
JACKIE CHAN ADVENTURES
JIMMY NEUTRON: BOY GENIUS, THE ADVENTURES OF
KIM POSSIBLE
LILO & STITCH: THE SERIES
LIZZIE MCGUIRE
LIZZIE MCGUIRE MOVIE, THE
MALCOLM IN THE MIDDLE
POWER RANGERS: DINO THUNDER
POWER RANGERS: NINJA STORM
PRINCESS DIARIES 2, THE
RAVE MASTER
SHREK 2
SIMPLE LIFE, THE
SPONGEBOB SQUAREPANTS
SPY KIDS 2
SPY KIDS 3-D: GAME OVER
TEENAGE MUTANT NINJA TURTLES
THAT'S SO RAVEN
TOTALLY SPIES
TRANSFORMERS: ARMADA
TRANSFORMERS: ENERGON

NOVELS

CLAMP SCHOOL PARANORMAL INVESTIGATORS
SAILOR MOON
SLAYERS

ART BOOKS

ART OF CARDCAPTOR SAKURA
ART OF MAGIC KNIGHT RAYEARTH, THE
PEACH: MIWA UEDA ILLUSTRATIONS

ANIME GUIDES

COWBOY BEBOP
GUNDAM TECHNICAL MANUALS
SAILOR MOON SCOUT GUIDES

TOKYOPOP KIDS

STRAY SHEEP

You want it? We got it!
A full range of TOKYOPOP
products are available now at:
www.TOKYOPOP.com/shop

09.21.04Y

TOKYOPOP
.:HOME .:ACCOUNT .:RELEASE CALENDAR .:BROWSE .:SHOPPING CART .:CHECK OUT
.: LOG IN
Welcome!
Sign in
.: SHOPPING CART
Rave Master Volume 8(1)
Princess Ai Volume 1(1)
Gundam Technical Manuals 08th MS Team(1)
Sgt. Frog Volume 1(1)
Subtotal: $33.96
View Cart Checkout
.: BEST SELLERS
Fruits Basket
A.I. Love You
Sgt. Frog
Saiyuki
.: BLOWOUT BIN
Gundam T. Man.: GWing
Gundam T. Man.: 08th
Gundam T. Man.: Stardust
Gundam T. Man.: Char's
.: SHOP BY GENRE
ACTION
HORROR
DRAMA
ROMANCE
COMEDY
FANTASY
MYSTERY
SCI-FI
.: SHOP BY CATEGORY
MANGA
ART BOOKS
NEW IN FEBRUARY!
Alichino
BEST SELLERS
Fruits Basket
ON SALE 50% OFF
GUNDAM W
TECHNICAL MANUAL

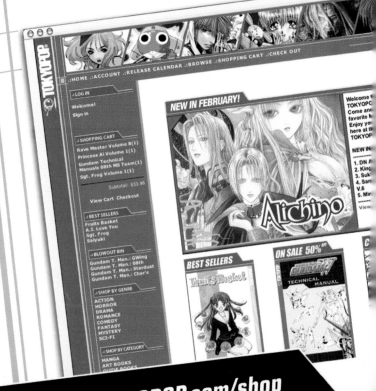

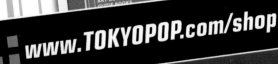